~ ROOTS OF STONE ~

ROOTS OF STONE

The Story of those who Came Before

HUGH G. ALLISON

MAINSTREAM
PUBLISHING
EDINBURGH AND LONDON

First published in Great Britain in 2004 by
MAINSTREAM PUBLISHING COMPANY (EDINBURGH) LTD
7 Albany Street
Edinburgh EH1 3UG

ISBN 1 84018 833 2

A catalogue record for this book
is available from the British Library

Typeset in Apollo
Printed and bound in Great Britain by
Mackays of Chatham plc

This book is dedicated to my mother, whose quest has been for knowledge and whose motivation has been love for those who are still to arrive.

And for all those who came before, some poignant and fitting lines from George Morrison's elegy for Rob Donn:

B'e mo thoil gum b'i'n innleachd
(It would be my wish that the means)
Gu cumail cuimhn' ort a leant'
(Followed to preserve the memory of you)
Do chuid oran a sgriobadh
(Would be to have your songs written)
'S an cur sios ann am print.
(And set down in print.)

The past is peopled by ordinary folk who were full of extraordinary resource. People like the Wolf of Badenoch's Mariota – a Strathnaver Mackay. Today's ordinary folk are no different and I hope that *Roots of Stone* speaks to the extraordinary that sleeps quietly beneath the everyday exterior.

Acknowledgements

I COULDN'T HAVE COMPLETED THIS WORK WITHOUT TODAY'S battalion of extraordinary people.

Thanks are due to my friends and relatives, and my work colleagues at Culloden Battlefield for their unfailing enthusiasm and support. Thanks also to my cousin John for his knowledge and his humour; to the Highland Council Archive Service for checking the detail in the end product; to my daughter Lindsay for the oh-so-fitting artwork; and to my father, for keeping quiet about this project until we could surprise my mother with the finished article.

Where does a book begin? I have no idea what the 'catch-all' answer to that question might be. I suspect every book's beginnings are as different from each other as are those of the authors who write them. I do know where this book began, however. One sunny afternoon in early May 2002, I was sitting upon the terrace of the Braeval Hotel in Nairn, enjoying a beer and the magnificent view of the Moray Firth. I was pondering what to give my mother for her birthday later that month and as I let my mind wander, I thought of what she had given us. I'm speaking particularly about the body of family research that she undertook, over the course of decades, for her descendants. That was when the idea of a book sprang, fully formed, to life. 'Wouldn't it be marvellous,' I thought, 'if I could shape the data that she had supplied into some form of gripping tale, with a beginning, a middle and a conclusion' (although obviously not an end).

Thus can a book begin. My next discovery was a big one. The old Glasgow maxim of 'one singer, one song' doesn't hold in the world of writing. Left to myself, it is possible that I may never have reached the end of this work and even if I had, it would have been a far poorer offering. The help, advice, support and suggestions from a vast array of people have kept me encouraged and enthusiastic, and I feel, strongly, that the drawings provided by my daughter, Lindsay, are a special and integral part of the book.

I was also greatly encouraged in my writings by the late Nigel Tranter, especially when we collaborated on the folk opera, *The Wolf of Badenoch*, in 1993.

In particular, I appreciated that long-suffering, but hardy, small band of readers who helped me throughout, by reading and patiently rereading, as I would tinker with nuance and issues of clarity, etc.: David K. M. Allison, Lindsay Allison, Kerry Allison, Dawn Allison, John Macdonald, Linda Turgeon, Caroline Munro, Yvonne Robbins and many others.

Further, very specific, thanks are due to the authors of those works from which I have taken short quotes to help me underline or clarify portions of the narrative: Sandra Train, *A Memory of Strath Halladale* (page 23); *The Ocean Ferry*, New York, Issue February 1922 (page 24); Donald J. Macdonald, *Clan Donald* (page 63); Hugh Macdonald (of Skinnet), *The Story of the Clan Mackay Family* (page 99); Peter D. Anderson, *Robert Stewart: Earl of Orkney, Lord of Shetland 1533–93* (page 114); attributed to John Colville, *Historie and Life of King James the Sext,* Bannatyne Club, Edinburgh, 1825 (page 115); extract of Earl Patrick's Trial (page 116); Ian Grimble, *The World of Rob Donn* (page 133); *Durness Genealogical Publication* (page 138).

~ ACKNOWLEDGEMENTS ~

Thanks are due to many of my colleagues in the National Trust for Scotland, for practical help and encouragement. Foremost among these are Stevie McLaren and Craig Ferguson, but also Stephen Spencer, Ian Gardner and Marian Porteous. Thanks to Christopher Duffy, William Potts, John and Ela White and Todd Fraser, all of whom have Culloden connections. My former colleagues in the Highland Council have also been supportive in many ways – thanks are due to Ian Murray, Robert Steward, Andrew Ferguson and Shonagh MacArthur. Encouragement from Bruce Dawson, Nairn Academy History Department, also helped.

Many people within the world of writing also helped me and gave encouragement and I would like to thank Neil Wilson and Mike Miller. Diana Gabaldon, Roberta Brown and other figures from North American literary circles also assisted in bringing this book to life.

I've left Bill Campbell and the team at Mainstream Publishing until last, as they are my most recent experience on this journey – and a very pleasant and professional experience they have been. Thank you!

Contents

Contents

List of Illustrations

Front Cover: House at Midtown, Melness
Back Cover: Castle Tioram

Linguistic Note

Much of the Gaelic contained in this book is in the dialect of the Reay country of the north coast of Scotland. Furthermore it also dates from around 250 years ago. The standard of Gaelic orthography has been fixed since that time, and fixed in a southern form which differs widely from the vernacular of the Reay country.

If any Gaelic scholars would like to pursue these linguistic peculiarities further, there are five pages (111–15) of in-depth grammatical, metrical and phonetic detail contained in the book *Songs and Poems by Rob Donn Mackay*, edited by Rev. Adam Gunn and Malcolm MacFarlane, Glasgow, 1899.

Introduction

THIS BOOK, *ROOTS OF STONE*, IS AN EXPLORATION INTO HOW REAL people and real history are one and the same. If there is a coded message within these pages, it is that the building blocks that history is constructed from are the lives of each and every one of us. We pull down books from the shelf and let them fall open at stories of heroes and villains and tales of derring-do. But, as we read of those long-ago times, it can be easy to lose the sense of the real people behind the action. Another way to look at the concept that this book covers is to think of the old saying, 'We're all some mother's son', and then reverse it. Those icons from the pages of our history books 'are all someone's ancestral grandparents'. They could be your neighbour's, or they could be yours!

The territory that the book covers is fairly straightforward – *Roots of Stone* is an interweaving of the story of Scotland with the lives of ordinary and extraordinary people. The sweep of 2,000 years of Scotland's past blends with the true story of a particular family (the author's), stretching back over these same two millennia in a fusion of history, people and places.

Although the territory is straightforward, it is the structure of the story that is a little more complicated. In an effort to help the reader to better navigate the idiosyncrasies of the narrative, that structure is mapped out here.

The Prologue stands somewhat apart from the flow of chapters which follow it. It opens with descriptions from Scotland's north coast – the Kyle of Tongue, the surrounding landscape and, in particular, the community of Melness. There is an examination of the concept and importance of the storyteller (the holder of the oral histories) within the Gaelic-speaking areas. These respected individuals were known as the *seanachaidh*. Moving laterally from storytelling to music and thus to the bagpipes introduces the reader to William MacDonald, born in 1891. There are a number of anecdotes about William MacDonald's life and he is firmly placed in time, both as the author's grandfather and as a direct descendant of Conn, who reigned in Ulster from 123 until 173.

The action then moves forward again to the birth of the author's mother, her early years and later perseverance when researching family history. It was her work, over a period of decades, which provided the basis for this book – the story of her family.

She gathered the oral material from Hugh MacDonald (of Skinnet), one of the last northern seanachaidh, and verified it all against written sources. What she found took her right back to earliest times. This huge vat of information was then distilled by the author and blended carefully with appropriate volumes of mainstream history, with the aim of creating a true tale with a spirited kick.

The Prologue, therefore, is mainly recent twentieth-century history and scene setting, but it also sets in context the direct lineal relationship of the author to Conn of the Hundred Battles.

Chapter One opens with a short consideration of the advantages and drawbacks of both oral record-keeping and written records. The point is made, however, that the information which provided the raw stuff of this book came via the oral tradition, but was subsequently verified by written sources.

The main historical story begins early in Chapter One, at Conn's court in 123. From this point the bulk of the tale is a straight line running through 10 chapters and 2,000 years in a logical sequence. The first two chapters are a fairly fast journey for the reader, through the first 1,000 years. This is partly due to scarcity of information and written records, and partly due to this book being the story of particular people, rather than an academic text. By Chapter Three there is greater detail, and successive chapters each cover approximately a century of happenings.

Through the early chapters the story covers all of the major events in Scotland, the development of the nation and the passing of generations in the royal line (including Macbeth, the House of Canmore and the House of Stewart). There are also tales and descriptions of many other powerful families who are also connected to the whole picture.

Things change orientation by the beginning of Chapter Six, with family lines taking a slightly different direction. The main thread of the story becomes centred on the north coast and the clan Mackay. That is not to say that the action becomes parochial. In fact, the converse is true, as the characters take part in the Battle of Flodden, the Jacobite risings and the Clearances. The arrival and assimilation of many other families – such as the MacDonalds, the Munros, the Douglases and the Rosses – on the north coast is also tracked.

As the story unfolds, the reader is reminded of how the main protagonists relate to the particular family line (regardless of whether the ancestor is hero, villain or merely observer). The historical detail is given strength and context by some richly descriptive passages and by the illustrations of some of the places of power within the tale.

Clarification is also provided by the genealogical tables in the Family Tree Appendix at the back of the book. These are of particular help when the author looks at some ancestors who are slightly off the main-line tree. There are some simple examples of that in Chapter Eight and Chapter Nine, when hearing of the wicked earls of Orkney and of the remarkable clan of healers, the Beatons. Table 4 is of particular assistance, because it helps the reader to make sense of one other interesting oddity in the structure of the book. While the story is straight line, through time, from Chapter One to Chapter Ten, there are two periods in the book where there is so much going on that the author chooses to introduce an aside. These asides are called 'Interludes', and the first lies between Chapter Three and Chapter Four, while the second is found between chapters Five and Six.

These asides give a look at some of the author's ancestors, other than those from the royal line. The three lines followed all descend from Fergus MacErc, and diverge from each other. They include the descendants of Thorfinn the Mighty, Somerled of the Clann Cholla (or ancestral MacDonalds) and the family of Malcolm MacHeth (grandson of Malcolm Canmore). Then the reader can follow the same family lines as they reweave towards a final convergence. We begin by looking at how the descendants of Malcolm MacHeth became the Mackays. Then we look at one direct descendant of Somerled, Elizabeth, who married Chief Angus Dubh Mackay. In 1413, Elizabeth and Angus Dubh had a son, Neil (known as Neil of the Bass) – a distillation of the MacHeths, Clann Cholla, Thorfinn's people and the royal line.

This divergence of these families from the main line, and then their subsequent reconvergence, is illustrated visually in Table 4, and the table helps the reader to make sense of a number of simultaneously occurring issues (e.g. which family line supported whom, and fought for whom, at the battle of Largs).

After the birth of Neil Mackay in 1413, the tale runs straight through to the present day. Chapter Ten covers the period of the Clearances, but also brings the action right into the twentieth century, and back to the people whose acquaintance was made in the Prologue. The chapter closes in circular fashion, with another look at Willie MacDonald: his music; his feeling for the land; his lineage from Conn of the Hundred Battles; and his passing, in 1963.

Roots of Stone ends with an epilogue. Here, the author's own upbringing and working life is touched upon, together with his motives for writing this history. There is a look at the renaissance in the Scottish spirit and the need for stewardship of the land. More than any of this, though, the reader can view the Epilogue as the Prologue's mirror image. It is the 'weight' on the other side of the scales. The Prologue told of the previous importance of the storyteller in society. The body of this book was created from the gleanings given by just such a seanachaidh. The Epilogue calls to the seanachaidh in each of us and considers the obligation upon us all to share the tales of our lives, as all of these tales are equal parts of a much larger story.

Prologue: Seanachaidh

TO THIS DAY MY MOTHER SPEAKS OF HORIZONS OF WATER AND stone and sky. Her green eyes reflect the northern waters when she speaks of the skylines of the Rabbit Island and Eilean Nan Ron. To the south rise the stone giants of Ben Loyal and Ben Hope, and keeping each from the other is the Kyle of Tongue, seeming – with its great sandy, silvery banks – to spearhead south between them.

Nowadays the 'new' causeway bridge of 1974, replacing the original ferry, stands blackly silhouetted against the silver of the sandbanks. Back in the first part of the century there would have been no such bold dissection of the view. The eye would have been drawn up and round the end of the Kyle, the same way that the feet might have to follow if you were to consider travelling east or south from Melness.

A long, thin place, Melness strings out along the north-western shore of the Kyle of Tongue, high above the sea. One of the most northerly communities in Scotland, it is what is known in the Highlands as a clearance settlement. Many of the people that live there are descended from those who were cleared from richer lands in the interior by the landowners of the north. Here, on the northern fringes of the known world, people were left to scavenge a living on small plots and gain their nourishment from the seaweed and poor crofts. Although the living was poor, the spirit was not. The culture of the *Gaidhealtachd* (the Gaelic north and west) burned bright with ceilidhs and histories of the people – the people of the land.

The jumble of sea, rock and sky enters the spirit. Northern light, especially on those long summer nights, is luminous. That light is ever-present in these elements. And so the people of Melness have laughed and cried, worked and played, sang and danced, and told the tales.

The tale-tellers and holders of the oral histories were called the seanachaidh (those who recite tales, the oral recorders; pronounced 'shennachee'), some of whom managed to tenaciously hang on until the late twentieth century. The time for them, though, is passing now, as the very air itself is full of radiowaves, transmissions and communication of all sorts. The greatest loss in the seanachaidh's passing is that the new information is drawn from neither rock nor sea nor sky. It may be of passing interest to know that a particular commodity with especially handy accessories is available from the shopping channel, but this doesn't tell people who they are, where they came from, their place in the land or the land's place in them. The seanachaidh was cultural bedrock. The liquid that flowed around this bedrock was the music. It flowed from voices, fiddles and especially the pipes.

There was a piper in Melness, a great piper and native of the place, called William MacDonald. Born in 1891, towards the closing of the Victorian era and only five years after the last Clearances emigrants left Melness, William MacDonald lived a life worthy of its own tale.

Leaving Melness in 1903 at the age of 12 and making that hike around the shores of the silvery Kyle, he headed east to Strath Halladale. Here he took up the position of herd boy with Colin MacDonald and, already a piper of promise, he became a great favourite at the fireside ceilidhs of the strath. His time there was documented in Sandra Train's book *A Memory of Strath Halladale* and it was obviously not just his piping he was known for, as the book had this to say about him:

> Old Uncle Colin had a housekeeper and a boy to help him, though the young lad Willie was more interested in the ceilidh houses where he could practise on the fiddle and the chanter than in herding sheep or cattle. Indeed one Saturday evening he decided to play a trick on the old man in order to extend by an hour or two his evening's fun. So he put the clock back, hoping that his master would fail to notice. At first his plan worked well; indeed that evening a kindly lady, Barbara MacDonald from the other side of the river, came to visit [. . .] The hours ticked by, many an anecdote was recalled [. . .] Suddenly a loud knocking came to the door and a man's voice called out in Gaelic, 'Don't you know what hour it is? It's the Sabbath morning.' It was the lady's husband . . . fearing for her safety as she had to cross the river, he had set out to meet her. The two within were amazed and astounded to discover that indeed it was long after midnight and soon the part of the herd boy in the night's mischief was recognised.

William MacDonald later became a piper in the band of the Scots Guards and saw active service in the First World War. Invalided home following a gas attack and severe wounding, Willie became employed in Inverness and continued to learn more, particularly in the area of the *piobaireachd*, the 'highest' and most complex form of bagpipe music. He soon reached the front rank of the piping world and won many prizes in competitive piping. He thus became a master on his famous three-quarter-sized pipes and was also pipe sergeant for a considerable time with the Lovat Scouts. As his skill increased, so did interest in his services. For years he taught piping during winters throughout the Island of Skye, temporarily taking a house there. In this he was employed and paid by the Piobaireachd Society of London. On one occasion at least he made it across the Atlantic. The story of this transatlantic foray, as written in *The Ocean Ferry*, New York, February 1922, is a joy in itself.

> MacDonald, who is companion and private piper to Francis Grant, a retired official of Inverness, was coming to the United States with his employer for a bit of a holiday. They travelled entirely as private individuals not wishing to attract attention. Alas for their plans!
>
> As the *Cedric* made her berth, it was clear the piping of William MacDonald had reached across America. The piper stepped into the full glare of the limelight of publicity as he came down the gangplank. Reporters and photographers saw him as a novelty. Movie men filmed him. In a day or two he was walking across the silver screen in the leading moving-picture houses of New York. In a week he was across the continent. Persons in society took up William MacDonald, the piper, and he played for them. One such event was at a luncheon of the Coffee House Club, a gathering of choice spirits in literature, art and music. After five crowded days in America William MacDonald and his indulgent employer sailed away again on the *Cedric*, on which they had reserved the same rooms they occupied on their trip to America's shores. 'She's good enough for us,' said the piper, 'and the White Star Line has treated us grand.'

Willie was fluent in Gaelic and a mainstay of many of the ceilidhs of the north during his life. He could feel the land beneath his feet and he passed a lot of that on to others through his dry humour. He and his people had been in the land, and of the land, since time before time.

The histories relate that Willie was descended from Conn, who reigned in Ulster from 123 until 173, and from Colla, who was Conn's great-great-grandson and Lord of Dalriada, the first major settlement in the west of Alba (Scotland).

Willie was also my grandfather and when 1925 arrived his life was about to be enriched – though he hadn't known that, nine months earlier. The morning of 16 May 1925 was blustery. When the weak sun rose, it was over a sea of unnumbered blues. It had already been light for quite some time, when, at 7.30 a.m., Willie's first-born child entered this world. Willie and his wife Annie named their daughter Margaret and she was welcomed by the whole community, many of them relatives, of course. Over the course of the next six years Margaret was joined by two brothers – Hughie and Donnie – and the inevitable consequence of that was the laughter, tears and lively life that siblings bring. Gaelic was the first and main language that Margaret spoke, until in 1931 the family moved 50 miles south to Lairg, to what had been Annie's family home. It was from this time, and throughout the schooling, that the use of Gaelic was progressively lost. Although the speaking of the native tongue was not actively punished (as it had been until the previous generation), it was, nonetheless, not encouraged.

The cycle of rural life continued, unhurried, for many years on that croft some miles outside of Lairg. But things could not remain so for ever. By the late 1930s change was working – both in the land and in the blood. Margaret was now an intellectually talented adolescent, working hard towards a bright future. That was the good bit. Not so good was the looming prospect of yet another global conflict. It was actually during the course of the Second World War that Margaret, my mother, began her medical training in Glasgow. That was a huge cultural journey, and at a difficult time, for a young girl originally from a croft on the north coast. It was in Glasgow that she met David Allison, another medical student, whom she subsequently married in 1950, by which time they had both qualified as doctors. I am sure that it was the same commitment and indomitableness that she showed in pursuit of her medical career (far from home and in difficult world times) that also helped her to succeed when she decided to research and document her family history.

What she found out over a period of decades is remarkable. And the information has a relevance beyond that to the people listed within it. The final picture is of a large family extending through time. But a family with its roots planted deep in the land and a family with more than a scattering of interesting people and interesting stories to consider. A family which over 2,000 years has danced in and out of the story of the land, to the skirl of the pipes or the clash of arms.

The universal relevance of this work is that this family is not unique. It is fortunate that my mother achieved such success with her research. However, most Scots both at home and abroad, if they were fortunate with the paperwork, or quiet enough to hear the land speaking through them, would find a similar genealogy. Much of the information began with Hugh MacDonald (of Skinnet), last seanachaidh, or holder of the oral histories, of the Clan Mackay. My mother then used a mixture of historical texts, clan records, parish records and information in both New Register House and Somerset House for reference and verification. It would not be altogether wrong to say that although my mother was looking for a family tree, she actually found the genealogical equivalent of Jack's beanstalk, and it was Hugh MacDonald that provided the magic beans. Sadly, Hugh MacDonald died in 2001, and although I view this book as principally a recognition of my mother's research and vision, it is just as much a tribute to Hugh, for his knowledge. This is doubly appropriate as their great-grandfathers were brothers.

In 1988, my mother prefaced her research with an explanation of what she had found and I include it here as it describes her good fortune in striking information pay-dirt.

It reads as follows:

> This family history goes back to the seventeenth century, but one line can be traced much further back. One of my ancestors, John Mackay of Strathy, was a younger brother of Donald Mackay, created 1st Lord Reay by King James VI. Lord

Reay's ancestry is well documented, both in *Burke's Peerage*
and in the Mackay records, back to Iye McEth, who lived in
the thirteenth century. Obviously his younger brother had the
same ancestors, so I can also follow my genealogy to Iye
McEth. It was a considerable challenge to see if I could go
further, and if so, just how far! Using various ancient
historical records Iye McEth's forbears can be traced much
further back . . . and then the ancient Celtic and Pictish annals
go right back into the mists of time. I have so far followed only
two ancestors back into the ancient regnal lists of Scotland and
Ireland: Iye McEth and Lady Elizabeth MacDonald of the Isles.
Maybe someday I will do others.

I do not mean to reproduce all of my mother's work verbatim
here, as much of it speaks loudest to direct descendants and
family members. I do intend to draw from it a number of tales
capable of illuminating the mist that is 'times past'. I will draw
from royal bloodline and I will draw from crofting hearth. They
will be tales taken from through the ages, sometimes of the good
and sometimes of the wicked, sometimes telling of grand
passions and the clash of armies, and sometimes telling of the
quiet satisfaction of an everyday task completed.

More than anything, this is the tale of my mother's family –
the tale of all the ones who came before and who can still be felt
in the blood at times when any deep emotion is stirred.

You know that! You will have felt it yourself at all of those
deep points in your life.

I hope that this book may encourage you to find out more
about those who came before you.

CHAPTER ONE

The Earliest Word

ANY AND ALL OF THE HISTORIES ARE TOLD IN WORDS. MINE IS no different. There is an interestingly divided attitude among some professional historians regarding the accuracy of the written word over the spoken, and vice versa.

I know that I have been told by some, who thought themselves expert, that if it isn't written then it isn't real. That is very clearly not the case. Have you ever been told what to get from the shops? Did you repeat the four or five items over and over so as not to forget a thing? Then what you did was create a mini oral history. But it didn't make your purchases any more unreal than if you had written out a shopping list, did it?

Some historians will tell you, just as quickly, that the drawbacks of the written word include full or partial loss, illegibility, misunderstanding upon translation or copying and the recording of a happening hundreds of years after the fact.

I would not care to comment too heavily on either view. I'll say only this: without the word there would be no histories, so let's not be too unkind to the word, however it comes to us. In the case of my tale, we are blessed throughout the bulk of it in that it comes from both sources: the oral histories first and then later double-checked and verified through the written records.

Consideration of 'the word' is important and useful here, because this first chapter begins in a long-ago time. If we are to wrest meaningful information from these early mists then we must trust the broad shape of the oral records we have available, especially when they are supported and strengthened by those few written words which we can track down. Our story begins in Ireland, in the second century, with the forebears of Clan Donald . . . my forebears.

The seanachaidh of the Lord of the Isles, Chief of Clan Donald, often spoke of the clan as Clann Chuin or Clann Cholla (the children of Conn or of Colla). This was due to the oral record of descent from Conn of the Hundred Battles, High King of Ireland, 123–73. Even 1,200 years later at Red Harlaw, this ancestry was part of a chant to fire the clan:

A chlannaibh Chuin, cuimhnichibh Cruas an am na h'iorghuill.
(Sons of Conn, remember hardihood in time of strife.)

Conn was succeeded by his son Conaire, then his son Art, and thereafter by his grandson Cormac, who reigned from 227 until 266 and converted to Christianity in 254. Cormac's son Cairbre Riata came next. He helped the Picts against the Romans, founded the first Scots settlement in the west of Alba and introduced the forerunner of the sport of shinty. His holdings in Ireland and in Alba were both called *Dal Riata* (Riata's Place) or Dalriada. What little is written of this period corroborates these events. When the Roman garrisons of Hadrian's Wall were taken away in 296–7, by a general making a bid for emperorship, the Wall was broken, a Roman writer telling of attacks by 'Picts and Scoti [Irish]'. Afterwards, one of Cairbre's three sons, Colla Uais, stayed in Alba to establish Dalriada as a sub-kingdom still subject to the Kings of Ulster. This is the other Clan Donald hero, and the clan are proud, too, to be known as the children of Colla.

After Colla, the line of Conaire ruled for a period, until

Eochaidh, son of Colla took over. He was known as 'he that was beaten by Maximus the Roman', which puts this action at about 377. Four kings later was Erc, great-grandson of Eochaidh, and father of the great King Fergus MacErc. It was Fergus MacErc who, reacting to the armed threat from Pictland, brought much larger numbers of Scots from Ireland in a sustained policy of immigration and settlement. This was in the closing years of the fifth century and is well documented.

Have you walked on the Lion Hill? It is a matchless experience. It is another name for the Hill of Dunadd, chosen by Fergus as his new capital when he decided to move the seat of the kingdom of Dalriada from his palace at Dunseverick in County Antrim across to Alba.

When I first came to Dunadd, it was a hot day. The wooded hills of Argyll had been pressing in on both sides as the car wound its way south. Then suddenly the world opened out at the edge of *A' Mhoine Mhor* (the Big Moss). An area of many square miles, as flat as a pancake in all directions, it is the flood plain of the looping, serpentine River Add. The heat haze shimmered, the china blue of the sky seemed to go on forever, and then I saw or felt it – the Hill of Dunadd, rising abruptly in the midst of the flats, yet near their northern edge. It looked almost unreal in the heat and the whole area resonated with the centuries of accumulated past that this ancient capital held within it. In the time of Fergus, the plain was ringed with settlements, habitations and places of work. The northern margins in particular still contain the remains of many pre-Christian monuments, temples and burial places.

The Hill of Dunadd itself tenses like a crouching lion on the flat plain, the living centre of the surrounding world. The Dalriadan aristocracy lived closest to the hill itself and from their place a path twists upwards, in and out of narrow defiles and onto the higher, broader terraces that make Dunadd a natural fortress, as well as a capital hill. The summit was originally ringed by circles of rock and earth ramparts, and it was at these lofty heights that affairs of king and council were conducted. Even today this rock fortress contains stones with a footprint, an incised bowl and the sketch of a boar. Oaths of loyalty by sub-kings (earls) would be made with their foot placed on top of a little earth from their home place scattered in the footprint – in effect swearing by the home place.

Dunadd, Ancient Capital of Dalriada

As I gained the summit and turned around, I was swept away. Not only is the past all around, but so is the present. Stretching away in all directions are breathtaking vistas of ancient Dalriada/modern Argyll, living comfortably within each other as though in a time-slip. This is one of those moments that speaks to both the fire and the melancholy that share the soul of the Celt.

To the east, clothed in woods, rise rank upon rank of mountains in ever-lightening hazy shades of blue and purple into grey. On all other points of the compass is the mix of sea, land and far horizons that is the western seaboard. There are headlands and inlets and islands as far as the eye can see. Jura, Colonsay, Coll and Tiree, Mull and a hundred others. All held in the western sea that was the main highway for these early Scots.

I returned to Dunadd with my own daughters many years after my first visit and found that the place had lost none of its potency. My children, too, had an opportunity to feel the land and sense the past in that place.

To return to the main thread of the tale, Pictland stayed relatively quiet at that time and in 502 Fergus was succeeded by his son, Domangart. There were no great happenings recorded within his reign, and in time the crown passed to his son, Gabran. It was in Gabran's lifetime that the lid blew off.

This was inevitable, really. After all, this wasn't an empty land that the Scots were moving into. There were already two distinct peoples within it, both of Celtic stock. Firstly there were the Picts, about whom little is known other than the fact that they were a fusion of earlier waves of Celtic settlers and their language was akin to Welsh. Although they filled the land from Forth to Pentland Firth, there were probably initially a northern and a southern kingdom, centring on Inverness and Forteviot respectively.

The second grouping, the Britons, were more recent arrivals and also spoke a Celtic language similar to Welsh and a degree different to the Celtic Gaelic of the Irish and the Scots. The

Britons lived in the south (Galloway, Strathclyde, Lothian and Borders), had been subject to more Roman influence and held a capital at Dumbarton Rock.

Then in 547 the new kids on the block appeared. Ida, a king of the Angles, seized Bamburgh and made it the capital of his Kingdom of Bernicia, which stretched from the Tees to the Forth. The Angles were a Teutonic people speaking a language related to modern-day German and English. These people were the forerunners of the English and, indeed, the very derivation of the name 'England' is 'Angleland'.

Alba was now an area for which the phrase 'to the four corners of the land' had new meaning. The land grab was on – there were four contenders and something had to give. The Picts attacked the Scots in force in 560. King Brude of the northern Picts invaded Dalriada, driving south towards Dunadd. Gabran rallied an army which met with Brude before he reached the Moine Mhor. The Picts were prevented from gaining the capital, but Gabran fell in battle. This was the beginning of 300 tumultuous and war-torn years.

Gabran was succeeded by his nephew Conall and the Picts continued to attack. The land of the Scots was in trouble. As if outside enemies weren't enough, there was dissension and internal feuding arising from those twin Scottish traits: pride and bloody-mindedness. Indeed Dalriada might not have survived without military reinforcements from Ireland and the arrival of an inspired Irish prince and second cousin of King Conall in 563.

This was Columba – in Gaelic, *Colm Cille* (Dove of the Church). It wasn't Columba, or even Ninian almost 200 years earlier, who brought Christianity to Alba, but what Columba did bring to the Scots through statesmanship and religion was unity and a moral authority. Columba's background has a lot to do with the significant impact he made in Dalriada.

Firstly, he was of the MacErc's bloodline – a great-grandson of Loarn MacErc, who was younger brother to Fergus.

Secondly, he was highly placed in the Irish aristocracy. He was related to the High Kings of Tara, in Ireland, and was, indeed, offered the throne on two occasions. All this also meant that he was possessed of a prince's education.

Thirdly, he had chosen to join the church and had become a monk and missionary of stature, training at the abbey of Clonard under Finnian. He went on to found the monasteries at both Durrow and Kells.

However, it was that association with Finnian that was ultimately to lead to his downfall. In 561, a quarrel began over a manuscript he had copied while studying with Finnian. Manuscripts were rare, the crime was considered serious, and he was brought before the High King, who ordered Columba to hand back his copy. He refused, civil war ensued between the King and Columba's Clan Niall and the King was overcome. Columba was appalled at the bloodshed he had caused and to pay for his sins he vowed to leave Ireland forever. His arrival at Iona, among his kinsmen of Dalriada, strengthened the church there and led to Columban monks being sent as far afield as the areas controlled by the Picts, and Northumberland. Columba himself travelled widely and made an overland journey to Inverness, where he became *amn chara* (soul friend) to King Brude of the Picts. The saint took a hand in politics again in 574, on the death of Conall, choosing Aiden above his brother as King of Dalriada. Aiden was almost certainly ordained on the Stone of Destiny (which may well have been Columba's own portable altar). He proved to be a strong and wise king who consolidated the realm and secured final, yet friendly, independence from Ireland.

After Columba's death in 597, the lands descended again into strife. Sometimes Picts fought Scots, Angles or Britons. Sometimes Scots fought Picts, Angles or Britons. The Angles didn't just fight the Picts, Scots and Britons, but also the Mercians, who lived to the south of them. And of course the Britons also fought the Picts, Scots and Angles. There wasn't a combination that wasn't tried – including internal wars within each of the kingdoms.

This constant background static of war creates centuries of half-seen pictures, not unlike a badly tuned signal: armies moving on the land; flames against the night sky; a woman's pleading hands; galleys burning at sunset in the western seas; a child crying; swords brandished against the sky; precious food trampled into the bloodied earth; images of pride, loss, honour and tears.

Sometimes, though, the picture clears and we can follow the most significant events in these troubled times. For some years towards the close of the sixth century the Anglians of Bernicia had been pushing farther north and west into Strathclyde. In 603, six years after the death of Columba, King Aiden decided to halt this Anglian expansion and met the Anglian army on the field of Degsastan. The battle was fierce and tragically for Aiden ended in the utter defeat of the Scots. However, due to the continuous warring between the other kingdoms, none were able to take advantage of the weakened state of Dalriada. The Scots were given respite to recover and were again brawling by 643 when Aiden's grandson, Domnall Breac, was killed by the Britons at the Battle of Strathcarron.

The northwards expansion of the Angles slowed between 617 and 655, due to their own civil war and the attacks of Mercians to the south. Even so, by 657, Oswy, King of the Angles of Northumberland, held power over the Britons, the Mercians, the southern Picts and the southern Scots. But the Battle of Nechtansmere in 685 changed everything.

Oswy died in 671, and in 685 his successor chose to invade the Pictish territory of Bridei. The Picts lured the invaders into the great swamp of Nechtansmere, north of the Firth of Tay. There they attacked and completely destroyed the invading army and slew the Anglian king. This marked the end of Northumberland's power over the other kingdoms.

Meanwhile, in Dalriada the removal of the Anglian threat gave the inhabitants the time to resume fighting among themselves and the kingship shifted from Domnall Breac's descendants to Loarn's descendants. Sealbach of Loarn deposed his own brother, then reigned until 723, when he retired to a monastery in favour of his son, Dungal.

I must offer heartfelt thanks that out of all of my ancestors my parents chose not to name me after this one. Apologies for this prejudice to anyone who is actually called Dungal today, but of all the ancestral Scots, I think that he had the most unfortunate name. Maybe that's why he only reigned for three years, until 726. The throne was wrested from Dungal by yet another family member, Eochaid, and for a decade all was quiet in Dalriada. This was probably mostly due to the fact that the Picts were having their own problems with internal fighting. Ultimately, a strong Pictish king, Aengus, emerged the victor from what had been a three-way struggle for the Pictish throne. This was bad news for Eochaid, as Aengus devastated Dalriada and, in 736, captured Dunadd, its capital.

In 756 Aengus led an army against Dumbarton, the capital of the Britons, and forced them, too, to come to terms. However, although defeated, the Scots still had their independence and one of Eochaid's successors, Aed Find, fought with Aengus's successor, Kenneth, in 766. When Aed died, his brother Fergus became king, but only reigned from 778 until 781, when his queen, consumed with jealousy, poisoned him for having a roving eye and a liking for the ladies. Things might have been different had Fergus reigned longer, as he had been a strong king. With his passing, however, a twilight fell over Dalriada. For about 60 years the successors of Fergus existed more as vassals of the Picts than as independent monarchs in their own right. The Picts and the Scots were thrown even more closely together in the ninth century, however. The Picts needed the assistance of the sub-kingdom of Dalriada against the most fearsome armed invaders the land had yet seen. In 795, the ships of Danish pirates breached the western seas, and the Danes plundered Iona and the west coast repeatedly over the succeeding decades. During the same period those other Viking peoples, the Norse, made raids and settlements in Orkney, Shetland, Caithness, Sutherland and the Western Isles. These savage attacks and incursions deep into Pictish and Scottish territories had the effect of throwing those peoples together in a joint defence of the land. The Scots were under attack on the western seaboard and despite being reinforced from Ireland in 836, still had to move eastwards and inland away from the exposure of the coast. At the same time, the Picts were losing territory on the eastern and northern margins.

In 839 the Picts suffered a crushing defeat at the hands of the Danes and the Pictish King Eoganan was killed. This gave the Scots the chance for revolution and, accordingly, Kenneth, son of Alpin and great-grandson of Aed Find, made himself King of Scots. Within four years he had beaten the southern Picts and in 843 he was made King of Scots and Picts on the Moot Hill of Scone. Just how he gained the Pictish throne is unclear and written background is thin, but it may have been through an intermarriage by his grandfather. The Stone of Inauguration had been taken from Dalriada, so that this Kenneth MacAlpin could make his marriage to both the land and the people he ruled, while seated upon it. In this way, the Stone of Destiny featured in the birth of the new joint kingdom of Alba.

The people described in Chapter One are illustrated by Table 1, pages 151 and 152.

CHAPTER TWO

The Forging of Alba's Nationhood

THE OLD NAME FOR BRITAIN WAS ALBION. IT WAS THE Romans who changed that. They latinised the name to *Brittania* (the land of the *Brittones*, or Britons). After that the name *Alba* was used to describe just the northern (non-Roman) part of Britain, north of the Roman wall. At first it was only a term of general identification and then, after the enthroning of Kenneth MacAlpin, it became the name of the new joint kingdom of the Picts and the Scots. Even today it is the Gaelic name for Scotland.

This new kingdom was, at first, a fragile construct. A Scots king in Pictland was a new concept.

How did Kenneth MacAlpin gain this joint throne? Was he the shrewd saviour of two peoples, building on their combined strength to bring victory against the Scandinavian invader? Did he wade in the blood of a whole tier of Pictish aristocracy, whom he allegedly murdered, to secure the throne? Or was it a little bit of both? Considering the harshness of life in the ninth century, I think that this last is the most likely. But we don't know for sure.

Written sources for this pivotal episode add up to only three or four lines of text. However, one of Ireland's lost tales was called 'The Treachery of Scone'. Drawing on this, Giraldus Cambrensis (the twelfth-century Welsh chronicler) tells a tale of Pictish nobles being invited by Kenneth to a peace conference to discuss the succession to the throne. Their benches were fixed by bolts above secret pits, and at a signal, the bolts were pulled, dropping the princes into the pits, where they were immediately assassinated. This tale could be fact or fantasy, but either way the end result was the birth of Alba.

'Berchan's Prophecy' in Skene's *Picts and Scots* reads:

> The first Irish king who will reign in the east, after using the strength of spears and of swords, after violent deaths, after violent slaughter. The fierce men in the east are deceived by him. They dig the earth (mighty is the art!), a deadly trap, death by wounding in the centre of Scone.

The health of the infant kingdom quickly became more important than whether its origins were established through bloodshed or by kinship. The Scots did not destroy the Picts; both were Celtic peoples and culturally had much in common. They were linked by 600 years of shared history, since the arrival of Cairbre Riata in 240, and his later marriage to Oileach, a Pictish princess. Although there had been much conflict between these peoples over the years, it was a mix of brawling, feuding, intermarriage and grudging respect often found in extended families.

The Scots and the Picts merged successfully as Alba grew in strength. Ultimately Scots Gaelic replaced the Pictish Celtic language, as people took the tongue spoken by the king. This period of 'settling-in' sadly also led to the loss of the Pictish records. The reigning Scots had little interest in these records and so they were never copied, eventually disappearing. It would be a mistake, though, to think of Pictland as submerged by Scottish conquest. It would be more accurate to see these events as the joining of related peoples into one strong Celtic realm, in an effort to better withstand pressure from outside sources – from both Scandinavian invaders and the threatening Anglian kingdoms of the south.

Kenneth showed his skill for diplomacy in choosing to move his capital from Dunadd to Perthshire. The proof to the people that this was no temporary occupation was shown by the decision to permanently house the Stone of Inauguration (or Stone of Destiny) at Scone. He further reinforced this seven years into his reign by moving the remains of St Columba (contained in the Monymusk Reliquary) from Iona to the monastery of Dunkeld, thus linking a Scots icon and a Pictish shrine. These actions brought a double benefit. As well as strengthening his hold on the infant kingdom, it also put some of the most potent symbols safely beyond the reach of the invaders.

Kenneth excelled at generalship as well as diplomacy. He not only defended the land against attack by the Scandinavians, he actually took the fight to them, both on land and at sea. It is said that after quieting the north, he had the space and time to mount six different campaigns into Anglian territory.

He also bolstered the position of the ruling Scots by arranging a number of royal marriages for his children. One daughter married Rhun, the heir to the British throne, in Strathclyde. Another daughter married Aed Finnliath, King of Ireland, and a third married the Irish prince, Mael Mithigh. Despite Kenneth's two sons and these three daughters, it was his half-brother Donald who was considered, by age, to be the fittest to rule after Kenneth's death in 858. This Donald I ruled only for four years, but is nonetheless credited with applying the laws of Dalriada to the Picts. He died at Scone, and was followed by Constantine I, Kenneth's eldest son, who reigned from 862–77.

Constantine's rule was bedevilled by raids from both the Danes and the Norwegians (or, as the chroniclers described them, the Black and White Gentiles respectively). At this time two Scandinavian kings ruled in Dublin – Olaf the White, a Norwegian, and Ivar the Boneless, a Dane. In 866, they landed in Perthshire, spent some months ravaging the land, and afterwards withdrew.

Ivar spent the next four years warring on the east coast of England. Then in 870 Olaf and Ivar teamed up again to attack the Britons of Strathclyde. Dumbarton fell and Strathclyde was plundered.

The Annals of Ulster record the Scandinavians returning to Dublin with their 200 vessels in 871. Their withdrawal provided an ideal opportunity for Constantine I to bring Strathclyde in closer, almost as a sub-kingdom. Rhun, Constantine's brother-in-law became Strathclyde's king and would father a future king of Alba.

Six years later, in Fife, Constantine fell in a battle against a Danish invasion force and Kenneth's second son, Aed Whitefoot, took the throne. He, however, was to reign no longer than a year, being slain in the Battle of Strathallan by Giric, foster-father of Eochaid the son of Rhun. These two (Giric and Eochaid) ruled jointly until 889, when they were expelled from the kingdom. Donald II, son of Constantine, came next and his 11-year reign was plagued by major aggression from the Norse.

During Donald II's reign, King Harold Fairhair of Norway included Orkney and Shetland in his kingdom, and he was active in the Hebrides and as far south as the Isle of Man. Sigurd, Earl of Orkney, allied with Thorstein the Red of Dublin and together they took over Caithness, Sutherland and parts of Ross and Moray. And finally, after all his years of Norse troubles, Donald met his end at their hand in battle near Dunnottar in 900.

Constantine II, son of Aed, became king and reigned for 43 years. He was a strong supporter of the Columban church and he, in turn, felt supported in battle by the spirit of St Columba. The people of Alba saw Constantine's long reign as a period of prosperity, despite intermittent raiding by the Scandinavians. Throughout most of this period the King was seen as fortunate in battle, favoured by the clergy and the provider of harvest and plenty. In 925, Athelstan came to the throne of England. His early reign was marked by wars with the Danes and Norse. Guthfrith, Viking king of York, was expelled and took shelter with Constantine II.

This put considerable diplomatic strain on Athelstan and in 934 he invaded Alba, and stayed for three years, undertaking looting and devastation. Constantine itched to avenge these acts, and allied with the Vikings. In 937, they invaded England with over 600 ships. Battle was joined, in the area of the Solway, and resulted in a terrible defeat for Constantine. Athelstan didn't follow through on his victory however – he became seriously ill, and died in 939.

At the end of his reign King Constantine had grown old and tired. Seeking peace away from the affairs of state, he vacated his throne in 943, giving the kingship not to his own son Indulf, but rather to Donald II's son, Malcolm I. Thus the kingship shifted stems again in the royal house. This is a complex issue, and probably worthy of a fuller explanation.

At this stage in the story of the people of the land, kings were appointed by 'tanistry'. At one point I was as ignorant of tanistry as I had been about seanachaidh. In this case it was my father rather than my mother who enlightened me as to the word's meaning. I had waited until one day when we were out hill walking together before broaching the subject. Of course, being an awkward adolescent at the time, I had asked when we were alone in case the answer would embarrass me or would involve dubious practices which I shouldn't have been asking about. I thought it might be something to do with leather (perhaps legal and, then again, perhaps not), but I was wrong.

A 'tanist', or successor to the king, was named from among a specific group of relatives. Chosen while the current monarch still reigned, he was usually a nephew or a cousin. He was chosen on the basis of ability, age and health. Since we know that no early king after Donald I was succeeded by his brother, the order of succession, or rule of tanistry, seems to indicate that kingship alternated between the two main stems of the royal house (in other words, the senior member of the alternate stem could expect to succeed by right). There was also a geographical tension, as one of these branches came to draw its power from Moray and the other from Atholl.

The main downsides to tanistry, however, were intrigue and murder. Despite, and indeed perhaps partly because of, Malcolm II's obsession to move towards dynastic succession, murder claimed ten out of the fourteen kings who ruled between 943 and 1097.

Malcolm I was called upon to deal with both internal and external aggressors during his reign and had to quell an uprising in Moray early on. Some years later, in 952, he also fought alongside Britons and English against the Vikings. It was two years later that he was slain by treachery, again in Moray, and quite possibly by the family of Cellach, whom he had dispatched in the earlier uprising.

Indulf, son of Constantine II, reigned from 954 until 962 and seems to have been considered a good king and a credit to the memory of his father. He also gained the name Indulf the Aggressor, due to his successes in battle against the Scandinavians on the eastern coasts. He fell in a skirmish against these Vikings at Invercullen. King Dubh (Duff) followed, but was murdered within four years in Forres.

Indulf's son, King Culen, succeeded Dubh. He seems to have suffered from the same family failing as Fergus back in 781 – a roving eye and a liking for the ladies. Also, like Fergus, this turned out to be fatal, as the father of a young lassie allegedly wronged by Culen burned down the house in which the King slept, so ending the sad story in 971. If a moral attaches to this tale it could be 'Those who play with fire get burned' or 'If you can't be good be careful', but the one I think bears consideration is 'The more things change the more they stay the same'.

King Kenneth II was the next to take the throne. His reign was considered good for his people. He agreed a treaty of mutual defence with King Edgar of England, who was so keen to recruit allies to fight against the Vikings that, as well as gold and gems, he gave Kenneth the area of Lothian. A major Danish invasion of western Alba was defeated in 986, after which the rest of Kenneth's reign was quieter, the main unrest coming from the raids of Sigurd, Earl of Orkney, in the north.

Kenneth II was assassinated in Angus in 995 by Finella of Angus, whose son he had killed. After Kenneth II's death, Constantine the Bald (Constantine III), son of Culen, became king. He only lasted about a year and a half before being killed in battle. Kenneth III, son of Dubh, took the throne in 997 and reigned, together with his son Giric II, for eight years. They both fell in battle near Crieff in 1005, fighting against the man who was, in one long reign, named saviour, father and destroyer.

That man was to become Malcolm II before the year was out . . .

Malcolm was the son of Kenneth II and by this was also the cousin of Kenneth III and Giric II, slain by Malcolm's army on the field at Monzievaird. Malcolm wanted to be surer yet of his succession to the throne, however, and so also arranged the death of Boite, Kenneth III's other son. Malcolm II was inaugurated at Scone in 1005, and the streak of single-minded ruthlessness that he showed on his path to the throne stood him in good stead. He reigned for nearly 30 years, and proved to be an able general, as well as an uncompromising monarch.

England was in dire straits. Ruled by Ethelred (the Unready), the country had been torn apart by successive waves of Norse and Danish invaders. Fighting was fiercest in East Anglia, Kent and Sussex. Nobody's fool, Malcolm II decided that this might be an ideal time to add Northumberland to the kingdom of Alba. He crossed the Tweed in 1006 and led his large army south. However, he was heavily defeated by the Northumbrians at Durham and, on this occasion, had to withdraw north again.

Malcolm spent the next few years consolidating his position and attending to his own Norse problems. He had two daughters and no sons. One of these daughters he married to Earl Sigurd of Orkney, and the other, Bethoc, he married to Crinan, Lay Abbot of Dunkeld and powerful noble in the House of Atholl.

Sigurd gave no further trouble to Malcolm after the marriage, even leaving his son Thorfinn in Malcolm's care when he went warring in Ireland. In 1014, the Norsemen in Ireland were fully and finally defeated by Celts at the Battle of Clontarf and it was there that Sigurd fell. Malcolm then appointed Thorfinn Earl of Caithness and Sutherland. An earl, moreover, appointed by him and not by Norway – thus resuming control of the far north.

In England, however, the Scandinavians were still in the ascendancy. Their conquests had continued for a decade and by 1016 King Canute (or Knut), the Dane, controlled all of England, which, at least for a time, became part of the kingdom of Denmark. In 1018, Malcolm II again invaded Northumberland. His army was drawn mainly from Alba, but also included some Strathclyde Britons under command of the vassal king, Owen. Sweeping south, he met the Northumbrians at Carham (near Kelso) and there utterly annihilated them. This was recorded by Symeon of Durham when he said 'almost the whole people, including their nobility, between the Tweed and the Tees, were slain'. Although the very completeness of the victory would shock us today, it is, nonetheless, what makes this battle and its outcome amongst the three most significant in the whole of Scottish history in terms of the forging of the nation. (Of the others, I consider Nechtansmere in 685 to be one, while the other, at this point in our tale, is still 296 years in the future.)

Owen of Strathclyde had died at this time, possibly even in the Battle of Carham itself. As a result, Malcolm II's grandson Duncan (son of Crinan) succeeded to Strathclyde. The kingdom was peaceful for some years after Carham. King Malcolm reinforced his hold on Lothian by expelling the Anglian inhabitants and replacing them with Gaelic-speaking families from the north. All was quiet until 1031 when King Canute marched on Scotland, intent on further conquest. He was met, and stopped, by Malcolm, and a friendly treaty was finally agreed. With Canute out of the way, Malcolm now had time to think about the future. The kingdom was, at least in shape, starting to look very like the Scotland of today. For the first time the monarchy had control over the area to the south of Forth and Clyde, and the country north to the Pentland Firth. All but the islands of the farthest north and west had been reclaimed from the Norse. This kingdom of Malcolm's, this 'Scotland', promised a strong, united future. It was a Celtic realm and Gaelic-speaking from king to cup bearer. It should also be deemed civilised in terms of the Arts, with some of Europe's oldest and finest literature, music and manuscript illumination. So what went wrong? And how did Malcolm II come to be known as Malcolm *Foiranach* (Malcolm the Destroyer)?

I suppose a portion of the blame can be laid at the door of tanistry as a system. In the later years of Malcolm II's reign his obsession with dynastic succession resurfaced with a vengeance. He was determined that his grandson Duncan should succeed him. With this end in mind, he applied his old ruthlessness to the task of slaughtering all other possible claimants to the throne. Gruoch, a daughter of Boite (whom Malcolm had long ago killed), married Gillacomgain. They had a son, Lulach. Malcolm, perceiving a threat to succession, marched north in 1032 and burned Gillacomgain, in his hall, together with scores of followers. Gruoch, and the infant Lulach, escaped this terrible fate and were taken in by the *Mormaor* (Earl) of Ross – Macbeth.

Not to be balked, Malcolm II then killed Boite's son, and his grandson, the following year. Other possible claimants, too, were slain, until by 1034, only four possible rivals to Duncan remained. They could doubtless feel death's cold hand upon their shoulder, as Malcolm stalked ever closer.

And then everything changed.

Malcolm II died in 1034, ironically of wounds received while erasing another claimant's family.

CHAPTER THREE

Rewriting Shakespeare!

TAKE ANY GOOD STORY – WITH KINGS, POLITICS, WARS AND A love interest – give it the Hollywood treatment and make a mint. And that is essentially what Shakespeare did with eleventh-century Scotland. There was nothing darkly unnatural or odd about the Macbeth story, it was just more of the succession deal, the way the Scots were now deciding to play it.

The death of Malcolm II brought temporary respite to the surviving representatives of the royal house. There were five of these in total. The descendants of Kenneth III would have had the strongest claim, if not for the fact that these were Gruoch and her son, Lulach – a woman and an infant. Tanistry, with its philosophy of choosing the most able candidate, would preclude them both on the grounds of gender and age. Next to be considered would have been Macbeth, firstly in his own right as grandson of Kenneth II, secondly by marriage to Gruoch and his guardianship of Lulach, and thirdly by fitness, due to being the right age and ability. In all of these aspects he was best suited to have been the next chosen king. The remaining two representatives were the respective grandsons of Malcolm II: Thorfinn, Earl of Orkney, and Duncan, son of Crinan. Between these two, Thorfinn was pre-eminent as son of the elder of

Malcolm's two daughters. Also Thorfinn had a superb military record.

Duncan, son of Crinan, ascended to the throne as Duncan I. As outlined above, this would never have occurred had the system of tanistry still been operational. However, Malcolm's thrust towards dynastic succession was at least partially successful at this point in time and as a direct result the ceremony of inauguration, in 1034, was a 'Hello, Duncan' affair. Even though, as a direct descendant of Duncan, that puts me on the winning team, I still can't help but feel a sense of outrage on behalf of the rightful candidate, Macbeth.

So did Duncan do well? If he had then there was probably much that he could have been forgiven. Sadly, however, his acceptance of kingship seemed to coincide with a personality transplant. Little had been heard of Duncan throughout the reign of Malcolm II, and yet upon taking the throne he seemed driven to try to better his grandfather's record of martial success. This was, in general, ill conceived and even more poorly implemented, whether at home or abroad.

He began by marrying Sybil, sister of Siward, Earl of Deira (York). The subsequent arrival of his wife's Danish relatives at Court was not welcomed nor desired by the Celtic mormaors (earls). This connection to a powerful Danish House seems to have been the catalyst to Duncan's announcing a claim on the overlordship of Northumberland. This assertion wasn't backed up by force of arms until later in his reign and even then he probably ended up wishing that he hadn't done so.

In the meantime, he decided to pursue Malcolm's policy of removing rivals. Taking an unusual approach, he chose to target the strongest first, sending an army, under his nephew Modden, the Thane of Buchan, to take the north from Thorfinn! That army was utterly destroyed. Having learned only a little from his earlier encounter, it wasn't long before Duncan again attempted to attack Thorfinn, only this time trying a different tactic. He sailed north with an army transported by a fleet of 11 warships.

Thorfinn caught them at sea, and, in a fiercely one-sided naval battle, his dragon ships sent the greater number of these craft to the bottom of the sea. Duncan escaped south with the remnant of the fleet to consider his next move.

Given the setbacks that he had suffered, Northumberland was probably looking like an easier target for Duncan and he accordingly invaded in 1039, ravaging through northern England and laying siege to Durham. The Annals of Durham describe how Duncan was defeated by the strength of the city and then driven north by Earl Eadulf. Duncan's retreat was poorly planned and executed and it was during this long trek home that he lost most of his infantry and large numbers of his cavalry. His brother-in-law, Earl Siward of York, attacked Eadulf soon after, and, following a complete military victory, and Eadulf's death, made himself Earl of Northumberland.

The following year, 1040, Duncan again took an army north, this time into Moray – the land of Macbeth. With Macbeth being married to Gruoch and the guardian of Lulach, three out of four of Duncan's rivals were resident together there. It is also entirely possible that Macbeth's armed strength was not as great as Thorfinn's.

However, Duncan's recent military defeats also meant that his strength was badly drained. His final defeat was somewhere near Elgin, where he was slain in battle. Later that same year, Macbeth was inaugurated upon the Stone of Scone and took the throne which had, by right, awaited him since Malcolm's death six years earlier. He was favourably named for a king. Whisky is known in Gaelic as *uisge beatha* (the water of life), and this new king shared part of that name *mac beatha* (or Macbeth), meaning 'the son of life'.

This was the time at which his uncle, Siward, sent Duncan's heir, Prince Malcolm, south for safekeeping, to be looked after at the English court of King Edward the Confessor. Malcolm's younger brother, Donald, was sent to the Hebrides for safety.

Macbeth is generally described as a very favourable character by the chroniclers – quite unlike the brooding, troubled principal of Shakespeare's work. Tall, with light-brown hair and a ruddy skin tone, he was renowned as a generous king and, most significantly, said to have made Scotland feel 'joyful'. He reigned for 17 years (in itself this is an indication of a strong monarch) and appears to have ruled wisely. Both he and Queen Gruoch are recorded as having been generous to the church and the Chronicle of Melrose says that the seasons during his reign were fruitful.

But not all was sweetmeats and light. Crinan, who was both Lay Abbot of Dunkeld, and Duncan I's father, led a rebellion in Atholl in 1045. The rising failed and Crinan fell on the field of battle near Dunkeld. The years immediately following these troubles seem to have been more peaceful, allowing the kingdom to prosper and Macbeth to gain considerable wealth – shown by accounts from the year 1050.

Scotland appeared to be quiet enough that both Macbeth, and his friend and kinsman, Thorfinn, felt able to go travelling. It is unclear from the written records whether they went together, but it seems very likely that they did. If so, then although Rome was their ultimate destination, it was more of a 'Statesman's progress': they took in the monarchs in Norway and in Alaborg, and the emperor in Saxland. Once they got to Rome there are reports of Macbeth scattering money for the poor. Four years later, Earl Siward invaded Scotland with a huge army, thrusting northwards simultaneously by land and by sea. Macbeth was defeated in the south, but escaped to make his way north of the Highland line again. It is said that Siward captured the old kingdom of Strathclyde, where he put Malcolm, son of Duncan I, in place as king. Siward never brought war against Macbeth again, as he died back in his home earldom of York the following year, 1055.

Scotland from 1054 until 1057 was a strangely divided country, with Malcolm ruling in the south and Macbeth in the north. In 1057, Malcolm marched north and with the help of the

English king, Edward the Confessor, engaged Macbeth in battle at Lumphanan. Macbeth was killed and subsequently buried on Iona. The rift in the land wasn't yet healed however, as Gruoch's son Lulach was recognised in the north as Macbeth's successor. It wasn't until Lulach was killed, near Huntly, in 1058, that Scotland once again had one king only. In this way Malcolm III (Malcolm Canmore – 'Big chief') became king of Scotland. Assisted by an English king, and later taking an English princess as his second wife, Malcolm was signalling clear changes in Scotland's future.

The chords holding the land were all twisted in tightly at this point. An invisible knot in time, and the reign of this king was enough pressure on the knot to get all the strings of the land deeply thrumming with possibility and probability. It was a time of beginnings and endings, a time of sadness for the passing forever of a purely Celtic realm, but also a time of breathless anticipation. Europe had been in the crucible and what was emerging now from the confusion of the Dark Ages was a well-ordered and stable Christendom, a Europe with strong government, common feudal laws and codes of chivalry. The Normans were on their way – a fierce, vigorous, overwhelming race – and the burning question was: what would be Scotland's response?

Malcolm III is often described as a brawling battler of a monarch, but he was more besides and many of his decisions showed clever political forethought. He had been raised, from the age of nine, at the pro-Norman court of Edward the Confessor. He understood the issues stirring in the world. Although opposed to Norman military might, he was impressed by Norman expertise and invited small numbers of Norman advisers into Scotland. Two of his earliest such advisers were the de Brus brothers from Brix in Normandy. In return for their help, he granted them the lands of Bulden, near Kelso, in 1060.

His main aim, however, seems to have been to ensure taking Cumberland and Northumberland as part of Scotland. In order to be able to concentrate his military attentions southwards he needed a quiet north behind him. He needed a means to neutralise the Norse threat left by Thorfinn. When Thorfinn died, his northern empire included nine earldoms, the Orkneys and an attractive widow. This widow, Ingibiorg, married Malcolm around 1060 and Malcolm was thus assured of the friendship of the Norse earls of the far north.

To the south, in Northumberland, Malcolm's uncle, Siward, Earl of Deira, had died in 1055. Malcolm seems to have felt no particular loyalty to Siward's successor, Tostig, even though he was Malcolm's sworn brother. In 1061, Tostig chose to go on a religious pilgrimage to Rome and Malcolm took this as a 'heaven-sent' opportunity. He invaded northern England, plundering and raiding as he went. Contrary to his hope, however, he seemed to make no territorial gains. Then for the next eight years there was relative peace in Scotland, Ingibiorg bearing Malcolm three children before her death in 1069.

During the same period England was in trouble. In a decade of convulsive change, the loose-knit and newish kingdom crumbled under Norman assault. Harold Godwinson of Wessex was killed by William the Conqueror, who was crowned King of England that Christmas, 1066.

Malcolm's sympathies lay with the deposed Saxon heir to the throne, Edgar the Atheling. Edgar had led a number of uprisings against William and ultimately tried to flee to the continent with his sisters in 1069. Fate intervened and a mighty storm blew their ship northwards, where it ran aground in Fife. Malcolm took these exiles into his court, and it may even have been on their behalf that he next invaded England (Cumberland) in 1070. Again he harried and burned, but made no significant land gains.

Later that same year Malcolm married one of Edgar's sisters, the Saxon Princess Margaret, and his court became a refuge for William's enemies. Margaret had been reared at the Hungarian court where the feudal culture of order and chivalry was upheld and the new European Christendom much in evidence. As well as being highly educated, and determined, Margaret was also an avid Christian of Roman Catholic persuasion. Whilst this match pleased many abroad, it worried a great number in the Celtic realm. Blessed with acute foresight, the followers of the ancient Celtic Church saw in Margaret an unyielding and puritanical destroyer of their faith. William, too, was angered by the match. Unable to accept the growing Scottish threat, he invaded in 1072, forcing a treaty from Malcolm at Abernethy on the Tay. Malcolm agreed to cease harbouring William's enemies, gave his son Duncan to William as a hostage and recognised William as overlord, but whether for the country or only for Malcolm's English estates has never been clear. It certainly didn't stop Malcolm raiding England in 1079.

William I died in 1087 and Duncan the hostage was released. Malcolm, together with Edgar the Atheling, invaded Northumberland in 1090, where they were defeated by William II, Rufus. Malcolm and his son Edward invaded again in 1093 and were both killed near Alnwick in Northumberland. Margaret followed them, heartbroken, into death three days later, leaving five surviving sons who would quarrel and fight over the throne between themselves, and with others, for the next 20 years.

So how did Scotland withstand the Norman conquerors when England succumbed so quickly?

Malcolm was certainly recognised as a mighty warrior and the purely physical defence of the country that he provided was important. When that was allied to the political work that his beloved Queen Margaret was undertaking (anglicising and feudalising the court), it meant that Scotland had more strength and standing (prestige) within the new Europe.

It will forever stand as one of our more painful ironies that Margaret, who helped save Scotland from the Norman yoke, was at the same time the catalyst behind the decline of the culture and religion of the Celtic realm. The *Anglo-Saxon Chronicle* says that after Malcolm III's death 'the Scots chose as King, Donald III, Malcolm's brother, and drove out all the English who were with King Malcolm before'. This was Donald Ban, who had been sent to the Hebrides for safety during Macbeth's reign, and having learned to love Celtic culture there, hated the anglicisation Margaret had brought.

Donald was the tanist choice. However, Duncan, Malcolm's eldest son by Ingibiorg, had been trained as a Norman knight during his days as a hostage. Tanistry meant nothing to him, while primogeniture meant everything (including a throne).

In 1094, Duncan, who had been at the court of Rufus, marched north with an Anglo-Norman army. Although most of his followers were slain, he did manage to dislodge Donald for some months and ruled as Duncan II. But then Duncan was killed by Edmund, one of Margaret's sons, and he ruled jointly, with his uncle Donald Ban who reassumed the throne on the back of a Celtic backlash. Another of Margaret's sons, Edgar, was also resident at the English court. William Rufus offered assistance to him to help take the throne from Donald and Edmund. Edgar agreed and entered Scotland at the head of yet another Anglo-Norman army. He overthrew Donald and while Edmund was permitted to live out his life in Montacute Abbey in Somerset, Donald was not so lucky. Edgar had him blinded and imprisoned. He died after three years and his funeral is of note because he was the last Scottish king to be buried on the island of Iona.

Both Duncan II and Edgar had accepted Rufus as their feudal superior prior to being offered the military assistance that put them on the throne. They were each, in effect, little more than vassal kings. Edgar spent most of his reign in Edinburgh and seemed supremely unconcerned by the 1098 expedition of King Magnus Barelegs. In fact, he entered into a treaty with him, which gave all of the islands of the west to the Norse. This gave them control of everything from Anglesey to Shetland, including the peninsula of Kintyre. Generally, Edgar lived quietly and there is no clear explanation of why he died, in 1107, still only in his mid-30s. He had been unmarried and died childless. At this time the two youngest sons of Margaret were sent for. They had been at the court of Maude and Henry for safety while their relatives wrangled over the throne. Alexander and David, therefore, had been brought up in a court that was deemed progressive in terms of politics and administration and full of the latest innovations from feudal Europe.

Alexander I ruled from 1107. There are sources that suggest discord between the brothers. It has even been suggested that David threatened to take the throne by force, but hard evidence of this has never been produced. In fact, Alexander granted David lands in Strathclyde and the Borders in 1113. It was also during these early years that he may have had an illegitimate son, Malcolm MacHeth. We will hear much more of this man and his descendants later. Alexander, in the first part of his reign, seems, like Duncan and Edgar before him, to have been a vassal of the English court and king, in this case Henry I. He had married Sybilla, an illegitimate daughter of Henry's, and even led a Scottish army to serve with Henry in the Welsh campaign of 1114.

By the middle of his reign, however, he had moved the seat of government north again, to Scone. He began building a number of strong castles – such as Stirling – and, more than any other ruler from the House of Canmore, attempted to blend and unite what was best in both the old and the new Scotland. It is a mark of his diplomacy that he managed, without upsetting the Celtic Scots of the Highlands, to introduce some Norman institutions such as coinage and sheriffdoms. He was also a strong king and ruthlessly put down an uprising by the men of Moray.

Alexander I died at Stirling in 1124 and was succeeded by his brother David, who became known as David I. He reigned for 30 years, and we shall hear more of this in Chapter Four. His reign was troubled, however, by two powerful individuals in other parts of the country. Somerled, of Clann Cholla, became known as King of the Isles and Man, and his brother-in-law, Malcolm MacHeth, claimed Moray and Ross at least, and perhaps all of Scotland.

This is central to our tale, and so I'll tell you more about them in the coming aside or interlude.

The people described in chapters Two and Three are illustrated by Table 2, page 153.

The Castle of Stirling

The Divergence

Now, ALL THE WHILE WE HAVE BEEN VERY SIMPLISTICALLY following the main line – I suppose what could be described as the royal line of succession. But to do only that is to miss out on much that adds cultural richness and depth to my family mix. There are a number of lines that diverge from our main route which would repay particular attention. And perhaps most coincidental of all is that all of these lines re-twine at the same moment in 1413, with the birth of Neil (known as Neil of the Bass).

The earliest sideline calling for our attention is that of Clann Cholla, the ancestral MacDonalds. As the seanachaidh make clear, this clan descends from Colla Uais, great-great-grandson of Conn, and from Fergus MacErc. There are many illustrious names associated with the early years of the clan, such as the Norse forebears Ketil Flatneb (reigned in the Hebrides, 890–900) and Godred, King of the Suderoys and Man, supplanted by Godred Crovan in 1075. Foremost amongst all of these, however, was Somerled, first Lord of the Isles and sometimes called *Rex Insularum* (King of the Isles). It is my suspicion that he is also my mother's favourite ancestor, and so, as this book is a recognition of my mother's research, we shouldn't pass on before learning at least a little about Somerled's life.

The second sideline which we might be encouraged to follow is that of the descendants of Thorfinn the Mighty, friend and kinsman of Macbeth. Thorfinn had a son, Haakon and in due time, a granddaughter called Ingiborg. She married Olaf the Red (King of the Suderoys and Man), whose father was Godred Crovan (mentioned above) and grandfather Harold the Black de Islandia. On his mother's side, Olaf the Red was descended from Harold Haarfagr (King of Norway from 872–930) through seven generations of Norse kings to Olaf's grandfather Harold Haardrada.

Olaf and Ingiborg had a very renowned daughter, the Princess Ragnhilda, and (if you can stay with the story despite the complexity) this Norse beauty eventually became Somerled's wife. I will tell you more of this when I tell you Somerled's story.

The third and final sideline that I want to look at is that of Malcolm MacHeth, who was a grandson of Malcolm III and Margaret (through either their son Ethelred or Alexander). By coincidence, Malcolm was also Somerled's brother-in-law, but that isn't why I am highlighting him. Ultimately it is his descendants who will interest us most and how they assist in the spinning of all of these threads into one strong line. However, for now, Somerled and Malcolm MacHeth are so interwoven that we can hear more of Malcolm as part of Somerled's tale.

Somerled (meaning 'summer rover') was born about 1100. He was son of the Dalriadan Prince Gille Bride, who had asked for help against Norse attack from the hosts of Fermanagh in Ireland. Although Gille Bride fades from view as a player, Somerled, his son, is next heard of in Morvern.

There is a story, a marvellous foundation-stone story, that says that the MacGillivrays and the MacInneses approached Somerled to be their war leader. The MacInneses had lost their champion to Norse attacks and sought Somerled's help because he was of the line of Colla and of Conn. However, this was in the early days, while he was still a bit of the daft laddie, more interested in fishing than any concerns like loss of land or culture. So when the clansmen came to ask his help he had already been chasing one wily old salmon for days. 'No, no!' he cried, 'I can't come now, but if I catch this king of fish today, then I'll take up the challenge and lead you in war against more than fish.' The fish was caught and the challenge risen to, and that is why the salmon is one of the four parts of the arms of the Clan Donald to this day.

Somerled's first major battle was near the Sheil Fords in Ardnamurchan. He won a great victory against the Norse, by subterfuge. He knew he was vastly outnumbered, but (a little in the style of theatrical farce) he paraded the same company of men in and out from behind the same hill sufficient times and in enough quick changes of clothes that the enemy thought they were faced by three times as many. When Somerled attacked therefore, they cracked under the strain and ran away, losing many men and two chiefs in the retreat. Somerled is said to have married a daughter of MacMahon (Chief of Clann Cholla in Ireland), but she died in childbirth within a year, in 1125. David I sat on the throne of Scotland at this time, and he was very pro-Norman and active in the ongoing feudalising of the country. He was opposed by the grandson of Malcolm III, Malcolm MacHeth (of whom we have already heard). This mormaor of Moray considered that he had a legitimate claim to the throne. He was strongly supported throughout Gaelic Alba, and especially by Somerled. In fact, Somerled gave his sister, Bethoc, in marriage, to Malcolm, to cement the alliance.

Malcolm's rebellion ended some years later in 1134, when he was imprisoned by David I in Roxburgh Castle.

Olaf the Red must have watched the rise of Somerled's powerbase with some worry and certainly did not identify culturally with Somerled, who was half Gael. Imagine, then, his outrage when Somerled came calling on his daughter –

Ragnhilda. Olaf point-blank refused to even consider the possibility of a match. But Somerled was canny and decided to approach his quarry from another direction. Some time later, when Olaf was on his way north to undertake official duties on Skye, he anchored his galley briefly in a bay by Ardnamurchan. By a coincidence that not even Olaf believed, Somerled 'happened' to be there too. He had with him a follower by the name of Maurice MacNeil, a ship's carpenter. This Maurice swam in the darkness to Olaf's galley, bored some holes in the hull and stuffed them with tallow. The next day Olaf and Somerled set sail, but as they hit the big seas, Olaf's tallow gave way and his galley started to sink. Distraught, he asked Somerled to help; Somerled refused, of course, until promised the hand of Ragnhilda. After that word was given, Maurice the carpenter dived overboard and was able to quietly repair the holes with prepared wooden plugs. It is from this man that the MacIntyres descend: *Mac an t-Saoir* or son of the Carpenter. They were, ever after, close to the Lords of the Isles. Somerled did indeed wed the fair Ragnhilda in that year, 1140.

The next few years were characterised by Somerled's slow reinforcment of his position, extending his lands both on the islands and the mainland, and founding the abbey at Saddell in Kintyre. In 1153, he was again at odds with the House of Canmore. His nephews were the sons of the turbulent Malcolm MacHeth and this was the year of yet another MacHeth attempt on the throne. The rebellion failed, and Donald MacHeth was imprisoned. Somerled's position, however, was little altered by this setback.

It was Olaf the Red's death that same year which caused the next sea change in Somerled's policy. Olaf's successor was his eldest son, Godred. He, however, was so brutal that his nobles approached Somerled, asking that Dugall (Somerled's eldest son and Olaf's grandson) be proclaimed king over the Isles. Somerled agreed and then waited for the storm.

Godred had to defend his claim and so brought a host of

galleys north towards Islay to bring Somerled to account. The two fleets met in early January 1156 near Islay's north-west coast and after a night-long battle with no clear victor, an agreement was reached that divided the Isles between them. The details became unimportant, however, as two years later Somerled invaded the Isle of Man with a fleet of 53 ships and completely defeated Godred, who retreated permanently, to Norway.

This victory over Godred, followed in 1159 with a major treaty between Somerled and King Malcolm IV, assured the country five years of relative peace. The same treaty also led to the release of Donald MacHeth, who had been imprisoned since the latest uprising.

Somerled now had the time to enjoy his wife, sons and realm (if we can call it that). And why not?

Somerled held the Isles for the crown of Norway and his mainland holdings for the King of Scots, but they were both far away. He had, within four decades, led the Clann Cholla from a life of oppression by the Norse to a position of pre-eminence on the western seaboard. Not for nothing was he called Rex Insularum; he was a quasi-independent prince following the Norse tradition in the Islands.

Malcolm IV, meantime, was continuing with the great work of his family. He spent these years of peace Normanising and feudalising significant areas in both Moray and Galloway. This included introducing Norman and Saxon incomers, who, in turn, displaced many local inhabitants. Somerled, in defence of Gaeldom, took a fleet south in 1164 to threaten King Malcolm. It has been asserted by some that this was not a voyage of conquest, even though he had 160 galleys with him. It is thought that his main aim was to remove some of the pressure from Moray and Galloway, which were viewed by him very much as Celtic neighbours.

The fleet sailed up the Firth of Clyde and the army camped near Renfrew. Somerled was murdered in his tent that night by a page, who it was rumoured was paid by Malcolm IV. One report suggests that Somerled was buried in Iona, but the clan has always said that he rests in the abbey of Saddell.

After Somerled's death by treachery in 1164, the dynasty that he founded endured for centuries and the seanachaidh in their *Clan Donald*, wrote the following:

> Somerled was probably the greatest hero that his race has produced . . . He wrested the sovereignty of the Gael from his hereditary foes and handed it to the Clann Cholla to be their heritage for hundreds of years. He was the instrument by which the position, the power, the language of the Gael were saved from being overwhelmed by Teutonic influence and Celtic culture and tradition received a new lease of life . . . Somerled's life struggle had been with the power of the Norseman, whose sun in the Isles he saw on the eve of setting. But he met his tragic fate in conflict with another and more formidable set of forces. This was the contest which Somerled bequeathed as a legacy to his successors. It was theirs to be the leading spirits in the resistance of the Gaelic race, language and social life to the new advancing order which was already moulding into an organic unity the various nationalities of Scotland – this new order was the ever-increasing, ever-extending power of feudal institutions.

Great heroes are easy to see. They stand out from times past like beacons, demanding recognition and attention. This, though, is a good point at which to take stock and feel the accumulated outline of the unnumbered ranks of other predecessors, the brothers, the sisters, all contributing to the rich patchwork of the people in the land.

Even against this background of a multitude of good folks and true, the three family threads that still spin most brightly in the land for us to see and follow, as this interlude draws to a close, are the family of Somerled, the family of Malcolm MacHeth and the royal family of the House of Canmore. We shall see how they intertwine in the Second Interlude.

CHAPTER FOUR

The Bruce Finds his Destiny

DAVID I RULED FROM 1124 UNTIL 1153, WHEN HE DIED AGED about 73. The years that he had spent at Henry I's court, and in administering his own vast earldom of Northampton in England, gave him personal experience of putting feudal policy into practice. So when he came to the throne he began reshaping the country of Scotland. Gradually he introduced the Anglo-Normans, giving land grants and appointing them to positions of power in the kingdom, as administrators, officials, military leaders and local governors. Robert de Brus – the ancestor of King Robert the Bruce – who was given Lordship of Annandale, came to prominence by this process.

The country prospered throughout this time, but, as we have heard, it was not an entirely peaceable reign. David brought great change across the face of the land and, as at any time of great change, not everyone took to it with the same level of enthusiasm. David, therefore, should be viewed from the same dual standpoint as his mother, Princess Margaret. I have seen it written that David may have been Scotland's greatest king. It is also true to say that the native Scots, especially those in the Highlands and Islands, described David's reign as 'invasion by invitation'. The MacHeth risings in the north were sparked by resistance to this creeping Normanisation, even though they also had a dynastic element.

David established many trading towns and the administrative framework of counties that he initiated persisted until local government reorganisation in 1975. More than any other single benefit, this brought uniformity under the law. He brought change to the Church too, establishing bishoprics throughout the land. This was a complete departure from the approach of the previous Celtic Church and took Scotland's religious set-up within the accepted bounds of mainstream ecclesiastical Europe. The religious houses that he founded across the realm were a financially costly exercise, but this was considered worthwhile by David due to the spiritual benefit that would accrue. However, even 300 years later, James I was heard to refer to David as *'ane sair sanct to the croun'* (a costly saint to the crown).

The religious houses did bring other unexpected benefits in that they became centres of learning and of the arts, and encouraged agricultural improvements. In his policy towards England, David, like his forebears, had designs upon Northumberland and Cumberland. When Henry I died in 1135, civil war broke out in England between the Empress Maude and King Stephen. David used this unrest to his advantage, warring across the north of England (and suffering only one defeat, in 1138), until Stephen agreed to grant him the earldom of Northumberland. The English civil war dragged on and when it seemed a benefit for Scotland to get involved, then David did so. The ultimate cost, however, was when David lost his son Henry, who was killed in the conflict in England in 1152.

When David died in Carlisle in 1153 he was, in practice, ruler of a land that stretched from Caithness to Cumberland and Northumberland. But he was leaving all of this responsibility in the hands of his grandson, Malcolm IV, who was at this time 12 years old.

Henry II of England reclaimed the territories of Cumberland and Northumberland, taking advantage of a young and naive

Malcolm by swapping them for the earldom of Huntingdon. The continued anglicisation of Scotland, and the dispossession of the natives to allow the king to give land grants to the newcomers, created much domestic unrest.

Fergus of Galloway led an unsuccessful rising in 1160 and then, in 1164, as we have heard, Somerled brought a major force to the Clyde. Malcolm appears to have arranged for the assassination of Somerled, which took place at Renfrew. The following year, in 1165, Malcolm died after a short illness, aged only 23. He was succeeded by his brother, William the Lion.

William's obsession with regaining the lost territories in the north of England led him, just eight years into his reign, to disaster. He joined the rebellion of Henry II's sons in 1173 and was captured at Alnwick in 1174. He was taken in chains to Falaise in Normandy, where he was forced by the Treaty of Falaise to do homage to Henry II for the whole of his dominions. William returned to Scotland, where he had to face 15 years of internal revolts from different parts of a kingdom stricken at the thought of the English overlordship that the Treaty represented. Firstly Gilbert, son of Fergus of Galloway, rebelled and was crushed by William, who then built a series of castles and burghs across Galloway to more fully subdue it. Next William decided to make the Highlands more secure. In 1179,he built castles at Redcastle and Dunskeath. Then, in 1181, Donald MacWilliam rebelled. He was a legitimate claimant to the throne, being the grandson of Duncan II and the great-grandson of Lulach. With the help of Harald of Orkney, Donald effectively took control of the north of Scotland for the following five years. He was finally trapped and killed in battle outside of Inverness by Roland of Galloway in 1187.

This was to be the start of a run of good luck for William – and not before time.

In 1189, Richard I (the Lionheart) suggested the Quitclaim of Canterbury, which involved selling all rights in Scotland back to William for 10,000 merks. This opportunity arose due to

Richard's desperation to raise money, by any means possible, to fund his proposed crusade to the Holy Land.

Then in 1192 the Pope ratified, for the first time, the independence of the Scottish Church, deeming it answerable directly to Rome and no longer part of the Dependency of York.

Strengthened by all of these circumstances, William moved to retake the north, manoeuvring against Harald of Orkney in 1197 and securing Ross and Caithness. Then, as in Galloway earlier, he secured his presence by setting up burghs at Inverness and Elgin.

William's reign was one of the longest in Scotland's story and although it started badly, by the time of his death in 1214 it could probably be judged to have been successful. Certainly, the Quitclaim of Canterbury, although onerous at 10,000 merks, could be seen as having bought a century of relative peace. William's son, Alexander II, became king in 1214, at the age of 16. All Europe was developing fast at this point, and Scotland was in the thick of it. Scots traders, Scots mercenaries and Scots scholars were commonplace throughout the continent and much respected too. Even so, there was some early unrest at home, resulting in Alexander having to put down the last of the MacWilliam risings in the north in 1215. He did, however, manage to maintain a diplomatic peace with England for the duration of his reign.

His first wife died childless in 1238. Later that year, to ensure an untroubled succession, it was agreed that if Alexander continued to have no heir then the son of William the Lion's niece, Isabel, would become king. The son was Robert and his father was Robert de Brus, Lord of Annandale.

This agreement was resisted only by the Lords of Argyll and the whole question became somewhat moot anyway, in 1241, when Alexander's second wife gave birth to a son. This change in circumstance did little to calm the lords of the western seaboard who saw the original choice as a further step towards Norman influence, and so, eventually, in 1249, Alexander readied himself for battle against Ewen of Lorne. This ended badly for him, because he died under mysterious circumstances (illness or infamy?) on the island of Kerrera, near Oban, and was then succeeded by his seven-year-old son, Alexander III.

This wasn't as large a disaster as it might have been. Even as a youth, Alexander showed himself to be both wise and strong. He consistently refused to swear fealty to Henry III for anything beyond his English estates and in 1255 he resolved the problems with Ewen of Lorn, who subsequently became a loyal supporter. The other lords of the west remained at odds with the crown, however, and some even became active against it, joining King Haakon IV of Norway's invasion force in 1263. There were reasons of duty and honour behind these actions and these are more fully explained in the Second Interlude.

King Haakon's campaign effectively ended in defeat at the Battle of Largs.

The popular folktale handed down from the Battle of Largs is that the Norse attempted to take the Scots by surprise. One of the Vikings cried out when he trod on a thistle and the alerted Scots won the day. This is one of the reasons given for the thistle being adopted as an emblem for Scotland. There are no other competing stories and so I am inclined to believe the tale – again recognising the power of the spoken word.

Although Alexander's rule was a good and prosperous one for the country, his personal life was beset by tragedy in the final years of his reign. His second son, David, died aged eight. His daughter, Margaret, died giving birth to a granddaughter, also Margaret, in 1283. His eldest son died childless in 1284 at the age of 20. Knowing the kingdom needed an heir, Alexander remarried in 1285. Four months later, returning to his new wife from council on a stormy March night, his horse fell from a cliff at Kinghorn in Fife. Alexander was killed, aged 44, and Scotland was plunged into a dark period of uncertainty, invasion, occupation and atrocity that eventually led to freedom.

After much heated discussion amongst the Scottish nobility,

Alexander's surviving three-year-old granddaughter Margaret was named Queen of Scotland. This was the famous, and doomed, Maid of Norway. Margaret, daughter of Erik II of Norway, was living in Bergen at the time, and there she stayed until she was seven. She sailed for Scotland in 1290, but took ill due to continual storms, and died a motherless infant far from home and hearth, on board ship in the Orkneys. Her short life ending in quiet misadventure in the Northern Isles was the death knell for tens of thousands of Scots.

The nobles of the land foolishly looked to Edward I of England to adjudicate the matter of the Scottish succession. They completely overlooked obvious evidence of Edward's obsession with power; how he had completely crushed and subjugated Wales; the atrocities that he had committed in Ireland; his expansionist policies; and the greed in his heart when he looked to the north.

When Edward came to the Tweed to proclaim his judgement on which of the remaining two claimants should be king, he announced himself as feudal overlord of Scotland. Not even then did the people revolt, for they felt it was a matter for the king, and as yet they didn't have one. Edward could have chosen Bruce, son of David's middle daughter (and the same man as chosen and named in 1238), but instead he chose John Balliol, grandson of David's eldest daughter. A cynic might suspect that the choice was made due to the relative strengths of the candidates. John Balliol proved to be a weak king and a good tool for Edward. During John's reign even the Scots called him 'Toom Tabard', meaning empty jacket, or puppet.

Edward heaped humiliations upon John, until, three years later, he achieved his aim. Balliol, who had been provoked to the limit, finally turned and rebelled. Balliol's ensuing treaty with France in 1295, is recognised as the first formal treaty of the Auld Alliance between the two countries; an alliance for mutual defence against the expansionist policies of England.

Balliol's rebellion was as unfortunate as his reign and it

seemed to take Edward no time to crush and utterly defeat him. Edward's huge army perpetrated the massacre of the town of Berwick (killing hundreds of men, women and children) and then undertook a triumphal progress as far north as Elgin before rolling back south, complete with three chests full of Scottish records, a Scottish king in chains and, allegedly, the Stone of Scone. Whether that famous stone was ever taken south, or indeed whether the original was hidden instead, has been hotly debated in many a publication and I have no answer here. It is telling enough of Edward and how he wished to smash the people's spirit that he even thought to try to remove it.

John Balliol was stripped of the kingship and imprisoned. Released in 1299, he retired to France a broken man and never again made a claim on the Scottish throne. His rising in 1296, however, brought to prominence two remarkable Scots. One was a commoner, while the other was the son of the Lord of Annandale. They were William Wallace, a country gentleman of Elderslie, and Robert Bruce, grandson of the claimant passed over by Edward I.

Both fought Edward I in July 1297. A number of issues caused Robert Bruce's faction to capitulate on terms at Irvine, but William Wallace and Sir Andrew de Moray went from strength to strength. Their greatest triumph was the Battle of Stirling Bridge in September 1297. Andrew de Moray was probably wounded at the battle, as he died soon after. This left the government of Scotland effectively in Wallace's hands (although in John Balliol's name) for ten months. But then came his defeat at Falkirk in July 1298. In all practical ways, this defeat ended Wallace's brief but glorious career as 'Guardian of the Realm of Scotland'. Indications are that he might have gone abroad at this point, seeking assistance from the Pope, Norway and France.

Surprisingly, Edward's follow-up campaign was ineffective and Scotland remained mostly free of his hand. As early as December 1298 Wallace's position as guardian of the realm had been taken by two magnates – Robert Bruce, Earl of Carrick, and John Comyn the younger, Lord of Badenoch.

Old feuds ran deep between these two and the tension was aggravated by Comyn's stance as a Balliol supporter. The situation worsened at a council of war in Peebles in 1299, with Comyn seizing Bruce by the throat. Acquaintances intervened and the quarrel was temporarily smoothed over. But the damage was done, and Bruce resigned his guardianship in 1300. Later, wishing to forestall the possible return of John Balliol, he submitted to Edward I in return for an undertaking to examine the Bruce right to the throne of Scotland.

Edward I campaigned in Scotland through 1301 and 1302 with limited success. The Treaty of Paris in May 1303, however, was bad news for Scotland. With Philip of France dealt with, Edward was now able to turn his full attention and military might on Scotland. He did so immediately, invading Scotland in force that same May. In July 1304, Stirling Castle surrendered to Edward (up till then, though, it had been the last castle in Scottish hands). The land was now wholly in the hands of English garrisons, commanders and sheriffs. Occupation and oppression became part of the daily expectation.

Then in August 1305 Edward created a Scots martyr. It was really one of his worst ideas and it was neither big nor clever. But he just couldn't help himself. William Wallace had been captured outside Glasgow and was transported without delay to London. There, Edward had him tried for treason (a charge without reason or logic, because Wallace could not 'break' an oath of allegiance that he hadn't taken) and sentenced him to be hanged, drawn, beheaded and quartered. Thereafter his remains were sent to Newcastle, Berwick, Stirling and Perth, as a warning to any other potential rebels.

Thus, overnight, Edward provided Scotland with one of its most enduring heroes – the legendary William Wallace, ordinary man and freedom fighter. I have read that the killing of Wallace was the spark that set the nation ablaze. If so, the very heart of that fire was Robert the Bruce.

And what of Edward? He, at this stage, was still proclaiming himself as 'The Hammer of the Scots'. Well, fine! But what he failed to understand was that when a hammer is brought to a mighty fire, the end product is likely to be a weapon of great strength. This is what Edward was, in ignorance, forging. This is what the Scottish people were becoming. A great weapon, wielded by the hero of the age, Robert the Bruce, against Edward himself.

And that weapon's downward swing began sooner than anyone expected. The trouble between Bruce and Comyn erupted on 10 February 1306, allegedly over Comyn telling Edward of Bruce's desire to free Scotland from English control and assume the throne. Greyfriars church in Dumfries was the scene for a heated exchange of views, ending in a moment of fury by Bruce, when, overcome with emotion, he struck Comyn down with his dagger. Comyn died thereafter and Bruce, too, was staring at ruin. If the Church were to excommunicate him for this act, he would lose any right to be considered for kingship. So he had to move fast. Faster than Edward and faster than the Church.

The following month at Scone, on the 25 March, Robert the Bruce was crowned upon a stone (perhaps *the* Stone, who knows?). What we do know is that he was supported by the bishops of Glasgow, Moray and St Andrews and the Abbot of Scone. In addition, he was crowned by Isabella, Countess of Buchan. She represented her brother the Earl of Fife, who would traditionally have played a central role, if not currently imprisoned in England.

It is as well that Bruce had moved as fast as he did to secure the throne by right. The rest of the year didn't go nearly so smoothly. In fact, disaster followed upon disaster and it is a measure of King Robert's strength and constancy that he remained undeterred upon his course. The day of 18 May saw him excommunicated by the Pope; 19 June brought defeat of his army at Methven; and for the rest of the summer he became a fugitive in the north and west.

The adventures of this hero king have become the stuff of legend – as recognised worldwide as the tales of Odysseus. For that reason, and as retelling these adventures in proper detail would require a whole book, I will restrict myself to giving you only the general shape of these times.

While on the run, King Robert became a firm friend of the head of Clan Donald, Angus Og. It was Angus who hosted him at Dunaverty, Rathlin and Dunyveg. It was while he was with Angus that winter, that he heard the latest black news to hit his campaign. Kildrummy Castle had fallen to the English and his brother Nigel and many companions were now prisoners at Edward's mercy. Edward, meantime, despite age and infirmity had been heading slowly north to deal with Scotland himself. Illness struck him at Lanercost, near Carlisle, and while he wintered there he received news of the prisoners of Kildrummy. I feel the need here to quote Tom Scott's version of 'Barbour's Bruce' – an account written within 70 years of Bruce's time:

> The besiegers of Kildrummy arrived, asking what was Edward's will with the prisoners. In one last rally of hate he raised his grim head and snarled at them, 'Hang and disembowel!' This utterly shocked everybody who heard him, that he, a man near death himself, about to cry on the mercy of God, would show no mercy to others, and they valiant men. But as he commanded, so it was done, and the blood of that butchery was scarcely dry before the old tyrant himself died and was buried. His son became king.

Thus Edward I died in July 1307, at Burgh-by-Sands. In the same period, King Robert had returned to mainland Scotland by way of Arran. Was the spider real? Spinning and respinning its web? I don't know. But if it was, it was either a Rathlin spider or an Arran spider. Either way, its example brought King Robert back again.

Seven hard years followed. The work was long and difficult. Conflict after conflict took place and always we find similar factors at work. Firstly the people of the land were inspired by King Robert's example and the force of his personality. Secondly, the Bruce's own feeling for the land and his ability to make it fight for him won him many battles. The castles of Scotland fell to him one by one. Some of these were captured by his trusted lieutenants – such as Douglas and Randolph. But others, such as Linlithgow, were captured by ordinary farmers who had been fired to patriotism by the flame that was Robert the Bruce.

Finally, only Stirling Castle remained in English hands and it was in an endeavour to relieve it that Edward II invaded Scotland in the spring of 1314 with the most massive and well-equipped army ever seen north of the border – records indicate somewhere between 20,000 and 30,000 men. Robert the Bruce fielded approximately 9,000 men, who, using the land and inspired by King Robert's leadership and example, smashed Edward's army. They pushed the English army into the marshes and river that gave this battle its name – Bannockburn.

This decisive victory cemented King Robert's position. In 1320, the Scottish churchmen wrote to the Pope to ask that he listen to no more misrepresentations by Edward II. This letter was called the Declaration of Arbroath. The most famous lines are:

> For as long as one hundred of us remain alive we shall never in any wise consent to submit to the rule o' the English, for it is not for glory we fight, for riches, or for honours, but for freedom alone, which no good man loses but with his life.

In 1328, Bruce was forgiven by the Church, and the Pope recognised his kingship. Edward III also recognised the independence of Scotland that year in the Treaty of Northampton. Robert the Bruce died of a wasting illness on 7 June 1329, but his legacy endures even today. How, then, was his five-year-old son David going to begin to fill that vacuum?

CHAPTER FIVE

The Wolf Loses his Temper

KING ROBERT THE BRUCE HAD SPENT MUCH OF THE LATTER years of his reign exhibiting brilliant statesmanship and undertaking a sensitive rebuilding of the nation. Although he was buried at Dunfermline, his heart was carried on crusade to atone for his sins and was eventually returned to Scotland and interred at Melrose Abbey. Even today, one of the greatest compliments around is to say someone 'has the heart of Bruce'. Sadly, as we have heard, his only son David was just five when King Robert died. David had been married to Joanna, the sister of Edward III of England, since the year before. He was four and she was seven.

This was a dynastic marriage. It was a move to ensure succession, and also to keep the worst of English depredations under control until David II came into his majority. It was unsuccessful on both of these counts. Although they remained married for 34 years, David and Joanna had no children. And only nine months after David's coronation, which took place at Scone in late 1331, England was again meddling in the affairs of its neighbour. David II's army was defeated at Dupplin Moor in Perthshire, by Edward Balliol (son of Toom Tabard), who had invaded with the support of Edward III.

Thereafter, things got a bit ridiculous. The claimants to the throne took it in turns to be king rather in the manner of a game of leapfrog. If not for the continuing loss of Scots blood spilt on both sides, one could almost have found it funny. Edward Balliol was crowned King of Scots in September 1332, but in December of the same year was defeated by Archibald Douglas at Annan.

David II was restored to the throne in December 1332 when Edward Balliol was ousted. However, just three months later, in March 1333, David II was again deposed, and Edward Balliol was restored. This was far from the end of the conflict and the two factions continued to spar until Edward III, who had been watching developments from Berwick, invaded Scotland in force in July 1333. David's supporters sent him at once to the court of Philip VI of France. The army of Edward III was met by a Scots army commanded by Douglas. The Scots were defeated with terrible losses at Halidon Hill, near Berwick, and thereafter Edward Balliol's seat was a little more secure on the throne. But not for long. Edward was deposed again in 1334, restored in 1335 and deposed for a third and final time in 1336. After this he retired into obscurity and as he never married, the claims of the House of Balliol died with him, around 1364.

Meantime David II, of the House of Bruce, was restored to the throne in 1336, but did not return to Scotland until his supporters felt it to be safe, in 1341, when he was 17. The year 1338 was good for Scotland because it marked the earliest beginnings of the Hundred Years War between England and France. What that did, in practice, was deflect Edward's eye away from Scotland. Unfortunately, the downside to this war between England and France came some years later in 1346. David felt that honour required him to answer a plea for assistance from Philip VI of France and so he invaded northern England. He was defeated by a force under Archbishop William de la Zouche at Neville's Cross, suffered heavy casualties and was himself wounded twice and taken prisoner.

David spent 11 years as a prisoner of Edward III and during

that time didn't acquit himself well. On at least two occasions he attempted to barter Scotland's independence in return for his own freedom. These proposals were repeatedly rejected by a people who were becoming disillusioned with their monarch. Robert the Steward, son of Marjory Bruce and Walter the Steward, was doing a halfway passable job as regent, and so the Scots could afford to wait for an offer that did not include becoming vassals of Edward III.

Finally, in 1357, a treaty signed at Berwick freed David in exchange for a ransom of 100,000 merks payable in ten years. This wasn't possible and by 1363 David was back at the court of Edward III, suggesting that in lieu of payment, if he were to die childless, his crown should pass to Edward.

We don't know how David tried to sell this idea to Parliament when he returned to Scotland, but we do know what they told him. 'It was there expressly replied by the three estates that they were in no way willing to comply with, nor in any wise willing to assent to those points.' In other words, no matter how hard, they'd rather keep finding the ransom instalments.

It could be argued that all of David's offers to Edward were conditional on David dying childless and that if we believe that he was sure that he would produce an heir, then his offers can be seen to be of no substance. But, whatever he thought himself, the truth of the matter is that when he died in 1371, aged only 46, he died childless despite two marriages. Furthermore, the business of finding the ransom instalments had to continue for years after his death. The payments only ceased on the death of Edward III in 1377, as they were viewed as a personal debt to Edward.

When David II died, the short-lived House of Bruce died with him. It had outlasted the House of Balliol by only seven years.

Robert the Steward, David's nephew, came to the throne in 1371. He became known as Robert Stewart, Robert II, and the House of Stewart began with him. He was already nearly 55 years old, being many years older than his uncle. He had also given his most vital years and service while regent during David's captivity. By the time of his succession his health and effectiveness were failing and so it was seen as vitally important to define the succession to the throne. This was all the more important as he had fathered fourteen children within his two marriages, and at least a further eight illegitimate children outwith. The last thing that the kingdom needed was more of the same unrest as the Balliol/Bruce seesaw of 1331–6. The King's declaration, therefore, to which the prelates and nobles agreed, declared John, Earl of Carrick (and his heirs male) rightful heirs to the throne. If that line failed, the crown was to pass to Robert, Earl of Fife and male heirs, whom failing, to Alexander, Lord of Badenoch and his male heirs.

Despite having acted decisively over the matter of succession, Robert II did little else with such conviction. His rule was weak and inefficient and contemporary descriptions say that Scotland was 'nocht governit' (not governed).

In 1384 Robert II was described as unable to deliver 'the execution of government and law', and so his son John was invested with the power to enforce the law throughout the country. Just four years later, in 1388, he too was subject to a removal of authority due to infirmity. He had been kicked by a horse in that year, and had, since then, suffered both a limp and poor health in general. The Earl of Fife was made guardian of the realm. He was already the Keeper of Stirling Castle and the national chamberlain.

Robert II died in 1390 at the age of 74. He had been incapable for many years, and had been known, in his latter years, rather contemptuously as 'Auld Blearie'. We are told that this was mostly due to his confused manner and bloodshot eyes in the later part of his reign. Speculation was rife as to whether the reason for that was drunkenness, over-production of children, or just sheer age. Strangely, however, when John, Earl of Carrick became king, in 1390, the Earl of Fife still acted as guardian.

One other oddity is that John was considered to be an

unlucky name for the monarch, because of the experience of John Balliol. Therefore, when John of Carrick came to the throne he resolved to change his name. Even with the whole book of boys' names open to him, it seems he could think of nothing more original than Robert (the same name as his brother). So for us, following the tale, we now have two brothers of the same name, one of whom is Robert III, and one of whom is Robert of Fife.

As we have heard, Robert II had a multitude of children, both legitimate and illegitimate. Four children of his first marriage, to Elizabeth Mure, are of particular interest to us. My family are descended from his daughter and my mother's namesake, Margaret. And we shall hear more of her presently. Meantime, her three brothers (who could therefore be properly described as my many times great-great-granduncles) were involved in a developing story of grandest passions. They were the King and his brothers, as named earlier: Robert III; Robert, Earl of Fife; and Alexander, Earl of Buchan. The tale that spun itself around these principals is one of epic proportions. The passing of time smudges boundaries and blurs edges. The teller of any tale adds a dash of their own heartfire, too. So I will tell you the tale of Alexander, Earl of Buchan. Alexander, also known as the 'Wolf of Badenoch'. But, in truth, bear in mind, while you join me in the tale, that he is the ancestor I find most fascinating.

Was he mad, bad and dangerous to know? Or just a man of his time, pushed beyond all endurance by a scheming politico of a brother? I suspect both of these are true, but I'll tell the tale and let you judge!

Robert II died on the 19 April, 1390. Following his death, the north of Scotland was effectively ruled by Alexander, Lord of Badenoch and Earl of Buchan, while the south of Scotland was ruled by Robert, Earl of Menteith and Earl of Fife. Robert III did not figure as an effective power in the kingdom at all.

Alexander was the King's Justiciar in the north and, like some quasi-independent northern warlord, was often called upon to legislate, sometimes to conciliate and other times to pass sentence. He is described as being a tall, fair-haired charismatic individual, somewhat larger than life. He had a string of castles throughout the central Highlands, stretching (so I have heard) from Garth Castle, just north of Aberfeldy, all the way to his main stronghold at Lochindorb on the borders of Nairnshire and Moray.

I have taken a boat from the lodge, and rowed out to the enigmatic Lochindorb Castle on the island, and yes, it is another of those places where the atmosphere crackles.

The Island Fortress of Lochindorb

Lochindorb must have been a very different place in the fourteenth century. It was the heart of Alexander's country. The roads would have been well travelled and at night the light of burning torches on the castle walls would have lit up the loch's surface. Pack animals would be plentiful, as would be the herds of livestock. The small folks would have their dwellings onshore, near the ferry to the castle. Out there, on the island in the loch, the castle would stand tall amidst the bustle. Its design is very unusual for Scotland, being a simple quadrangular layout, with four corner towers. There is an added feature of a massive curtain wall outwith the original quadrangle which, it is said, was built when Edward I occupied the castle in 1303. The castle is more tumbledown now and the surrounding heather moor of Dava is almost empty. Yet this place, this three-mile-long oval of water on the roof of the Highlands, still has a powerful presence.

So there we have Alexander. Lord of an island stronghold and leader of the north. His justice could be swift, and indeed it could be savage, and we would be innocents if we didn't accept that he did some freebooting on his own behalf. But he did seem to have had the respect of the Highland clans, which was never given easily and had to be earned. His domestic life too seems to have been generally untroubled until that fateful spring. He lived at Lochindorb for many years with a concubine of some note, called Mariota de Athyn. We are told that she was actually a Mackay from Strathnaver, and that together they had five sons. It seemed almost incidental that Alexander also had a wife, Euphemia, Countess of Ross, from whom Alexander held the earldom for life, even though he had deserted her.

In the south at this same time was Robert, Earl of Fife, Alexander's brother and the most powerful man in the kingdom. He is a shadowy figure, whose motivations are slightly less than clear, but he does seem to have desired the throne. Let's not forget that this is the same individual who would be suspected, 12 years later in 1402, of starving the King's eldest son to death in the dungeon of Falkland Palace in Fife. He would also be suspected, in 1406, of taking a hand in getting the King's only other son, seven-year-old James, captured by the English, and imprisoned in the Tower of London for eighteen years.

It is therefore easy to see him working against Alexander, whom he must have viewed as either competition or a threat. It was Robert of Fife who realised that non-consummation of the holy marriage vows was an offence which could be punished by excommunication, and that an excommunicate cannot be considered as a candidate for the throne.

Thus, before Robert II was even dead, the enigmatic Earl of Fife was already plotting to remove Alexander from the succession table, using the Church, and in particular, Bishop Burr of Elgin Cathedral, as his tool.

Repeatedly through 1389 the Bishop had sent warning to Alexander that he was required to return to his wife. Finally the Bishop appeared to decide that stronger action was necessary. The ensuing letter of excommunication, coinciding as it did with the death of his father, seems to have pushed Alexander wholly over the edge. Spring of 1390 was going to bring that sequence of events which would give Alexander his new title: Wolf of Badenoch.

Lochindorb seems nowadays very much the backwater, but in reality, then as now, it was a strong place, practically overlooking all the main routeways and busy Norman burghs of the Moray coast.

It was the ideal place for Alexander to gather his Highland army that May. He had struck upon the plan that a dead wife could not sue for desertion and he had heard that Euphemia was, at that time, staying in church accommodations in the burgh of Forres.

His hope, I feel sure, is that before long he could resume his life with Mariota at Lochindorb, untroubled by churchmen and ambitious brothers. He certainly managed to raze Forres to the ground, but of Euphemia there was no sign, as she had received warning and had been hurried away to Pluscarden Abbey. Almost without pause, Alexander managed to turn his host and marched on the Abbey. A poorly defended place, it fell quickly and hungry fire lit up the Moray sky. But here, too, the quarry had flown. She had taken refuge in the city of Elgin. Instead of this turn of events giving Alexander time to reflect on the foolishness of his present course, it just seems to have inflamed him further. And Elgin was no easy target. The cathedral was a place of great learning – often called the 'Lantern of the North' due to the light of knowledge that it provided. The city also had many other religious houses, hospitals, etc., and the whole place was ringed about with strong walls and gates.

It was here that Alexander took his army in June. It was a pointless exercise from the outset, as Euphemia had again been moved elsewhere for safety. Taking the gates, Alexander's army swept into the city, burnt down the town, the church of Saint Giles, the hospital of Maison Dieu, 18 religious houses in the college of Elgin and the cathedral. He was now fully and finally the Wolf of Badenoch, the man that lit the Lantern of the North.

This act of madness seems to have drained his wrath, because afterwards he retired in sullen silence to Lochindorb for some while. He was prosecuted and required, by his brother the King, to do public penance and present himself in Perth that autumn.

Upon making his submission he was absolved, and the excommunication was nullified by Walter Trail, Bishop of St Andrews in the Church of the Black Friars in Perth, in the presence of Robert III and many of the nobility. There he expressed regret and made financial restitution. Of his brother, the Earl of Fife and instigator of plots, there was no sign.

And so here ends the tale. Or almost. Who lived happily ever after and who didn't?

Robert III was heard to tell his wife he should be buried under a dungheap, with the words: 'Here lies the worst of kings and most miserable of men.' He died of a broken heart in 1406, after receiving news of the capture of his last surviving son, James, by the English.

Robert, Earl of Fife was created Duke of Albany in 1398 and ruled as Governor of Scotland from 1406 until his death, aged 80, in 1420.

Alexander died in strange circumstances, possibly in July 1405. Sources are strangely confused on this issue, but point to a natural death following an illness. Some accounts have him dying as early as 1394 and others as late as 1406. Does he lie in his tomb in Dunkeld? Did he go overseas, as penance, on a crusade? And if so, did he return? Or, most unlikely, was he taken from Ruthven Castle (the site now occupied by Ruthven Barracks) by the Devil, for losing at cards? An eyewitness account says yes to this last, but I'm happy to stay guessing! And Margaret, the sister of these turbulent and feuding heirs of Robert II, married into Clann Cholla, about whom we have already heard so much. With this marriage my family line takes a different route from that of the House of Stewart. How that occurs is the subject of our Second Interlude, where we also look at the re-twining of the families we met in the First Interlude.

The people described in chapters Four and Five are illustrated by Table 3, page 154.

The Convergence

WE SAW, IN THE FIRST INTERLUDE, THE LINES OF CLANN Cholla, Thorfinn and MacHeth separating from the main line of royal succession. We also saw how the line of Thorfinn later bound itself to that of Clann Cholla, with the marriage of Somerled and Ragnhilda. The other strands, too, begin to spin in closer to each other again. And as they touch, and begin to entwine, I am, in part, reminded of the process of making ornate Celtic jewellery. Threads of gold are taken and braided together to make a very strong finished item, like a torc, or a bracer. The essence of the process is that the end product is stronger because of the different elements in the weave. We have seen how the House of Canmore ended (with a young maid of seven years dying, far from home, in 1290). The wars of succession and the feats of Bruce followed, culminating in the founding of a new dynasty – the Stewarts. We looked at their early years, through to the internal feuding of the heirs of Robert II.

What is this of convergence though? What had the ancestors in the other strands of descent been up to since the death of Somerled in 1164.

The descendants of Donald MacHeth were again in arms against the King in 1198, when Earl Harold of Caithness – a MacHeth son-in-law – was killed in battle in Strathnaver. The family became less rebellious after the death of Kenneth McEth in 1214. Donald's great-grandson was Iye McEth (sometimes spelt 'Aodh' or 'Aoidh'), born about 1230. He was the first of his name to settle in Strathnaver in Sutherland and was chamberlain to Walter de Baltrode, Bishop of Caithness. He married the Bishop's daughter and she gave birth to a son, Iye Mor, in 1263. By name this son was, of course, Iye MacIye – hence the founder of the Clan Mackay. He was born in Strathnaver and the time of his birth wasn't a quiet period for Scotland, 1263 being the year of the Battle of Largs. This was not a simple conflict, as these were not culturally simple times. The country was wounded by split loyalties and the same rich breadth of ancestry that was a strength in peacetime was a curse in war.

The Mackays were largely of Viking stock. What would they do, faced with a Norse invasion? Clan Donald were mixed Celtic and Viking. How would they react?

In fact, when King Haakon IV invaded, personally leading a massive fleet of galleys, the Mackays didn't rally to his banner. However, Ruari, uncle of the Lord of the Isles, did lead some of the Clan Donald out to assist King Haakon. Politically there was no right or wrong response. Norse, Scot and Pict had been fairly well mixed in the pot that was the Scottish nation and all had held sovereign rights there. The Vikings were decisively routed at Largs, however, and were never again a cause of civil conflict in Scotland. As Iye Mor grew older, he was given land in north-west Sutherland by his grandfather, the Bishop.

This area that he was granted became known as '*Duthaich 'ic Aoidh*', which is Gaelic for 'The Land of Mackay'.

Iye Mor had a son, Donald, who was born in 1285. He married a daughter of MacNeil of Gigha, and they in turn had a son, in 1305 in Durness, whom they not unsurprisingly named Iye. Donald was the man who led the Mackays at the time of Bruce at

Bannockburn and this was when young Iye was still just nine years old. Indeed, in 1329, just before his death, King Robert the Bruce gave lands in Kintyre to Gilchrist MacYmar MacCay for the service of two bowmen in the King's army.

Throughout Iye's maturity, and indeed that of his own son, Donald (born in 1325 in Durness), their lives were marked by land disputes with the Earl of Sutherland.

This Earl received the Earldom of Sutherland in regality in 1345, 'settled on the lawful heirs' of him and his wife, the sister of King David II. In reality, the only child of this union died childless, before his father. The Mackays therefore felt that the superiority over Strathnaver was void and that the heirs of the Earl's second marriage were not legally entitled to the regality. Sutherland disagreed and pursued his case fiercely. In 1370, arbiters called representatives of both families to a meeting in Dingwall in order to consider both sides and make a judgement. It is said that all proceedings were leading towards a likely victory for the Mackays, which is the excuse given for the 5th Earl of Sutherland murdering both Iye and Donald, his heir, there in Dingwall Castle. In all fairness, we are told that it was not the Earl himself that did the deed. In order to keep the Earl at arm's length, his brother, Nicholas Sutherland of Duffus, committed the murder, and was then in turn pursued unsuccessfully by Mackay retainers as he fled towards Sutherland country.

The line didn't wither, however, as the murdered Donald had two sons – Angus (born 1345) and Uisdean Dubh (born 1350). 'Dubh' is Gaelic for black, and could refer to hair colour. Angus married a daughter of Torquil MacLeod of Lewis and in 1365 (five years before the murder of his father and grandfather) became the father of a boy – Angus Dubh. As he grew into adulthood, this Angus Dubh became a mercenary soldier in Ireland, a common practice at that time. He lived during the reigns of Robert II, Robert III and James I, and in 1427 he was the leader of 4,000 men. We will hear more about him later, but for now I wish to have a look at how Clan Donald fared through this same time period.

Somerled had many sons and one daughter. His daughter, Beatrice (Behag), was installed by her brother Ranald as the first prioress in his newly completed priory for Benedictine nuns on Iona. An inscription on her gravestone read *Behag Nyn Shorly Ilvrid Prioressa* (Beatrice, daughter of Somerled; Prioress).

Of the boys, there were several sons by unrecorded mothers. The eldest, Gillecoluim, fell alongside his father in 1164. Somerled's sons by Ragnhilda inherited the clan lands. As far as we know, their names were Dugall, Ranald and Angus. We don't know which was the eldest, as there is no record of the years of their birth. In addition, the law of primogeniture (inheritance by the eldest son) had not yet overtaken tanistry in the far west. Thus, despite eight and a half centuries of angst twixt Clan Donald and Clan Dugall, no one is any nearer to being sure of which branch is – technically – the senior branch of Clann Cholla. In reality, for our purposes it doesn't matter. Ranald, from whom I descend, found himself in all practical ways in the senior position. He inherited the core lands of Clann Cholla domains – Islay and Kintyre – and was popular on both sides of the Irish Sea. As well as being an accomplished warrior, he was especially known as a peacemaker. He was generous to the Church, founding two monasteries on Iona and one associated with his father's abbey at Saddell in Kintyre. Ranald died peacefully in 1207 and was succeeded by his son Donald. This is the chief who gave the clan its name – Clan Donald or MacDonald.

Of the other two branches, the MacDugalls eventually became the MacDougalls of Lorn, the implacable enemies of Robert the Bruce during the Wars of Independence, and ultimately became affiliated to the Campbells of Argyll. Angus's line didn't last long, as he, and his three sons, were killed in battle against the Norse king of the Outer Hebrides in 1210. Thereafter, his lands were split between Dugall's family and Ranald's sons – Donald and Ruari.

Although Donald and Ruari ruled different parts of the clan lands, it was a flexible arrangement which allowed them to join forces when it was to the clan's advantage. Donald was, through most of his life, the hardman of the Clann Cholla. War, weapons and wounding seemed to be the order of the day. As early as 1211 he raided Ireland together with Ruari. After plundering and destroying the town of Derry with a fleet of 76 ships, the pair went on to 'despoil' the whole peninsula of Inishowen.

Donald also got involved with the later McEth rebellions but, in the main, these died along with Kenneth McEth in 1214. The final solution to the McEth risings was when Alexander II came north to Argyll and the Isles in 1221 to attempt to deal with Clann Cholla for its part in the unrest. There was a lot of lip service and then, once Alexander had gone, life continued as normal. Alexander returned in force in 1249, but Donald wouldn't meet with him. The King then tried to recruit Ewen of Lorn to his cause, but to no avail. Ewen held lands and position from Haakon of Norway and was not about to jeopardise them.

What happened at Kerrera, off Oban, is unclear. Perhaps Ewen had plotted the King's death or perhaps a genuine illness carried him off, but either way, Kerrera is where Alexander II's reign ended.

After this time, Donald repented of the darker, wilder deeds of his youth, retiring as leader of the clan in favour of his son, Angus Mor. Donald then went on a journey to Rome, with seven priests, and gained absolution from the Pope. He lived out his life in retreat in the Abbey of Paisley to which he had also generously gifted cattle and coin, and when he died, about 1269, he was buried on Iona.

Angus Mor was therefore clan chief when King Haakon invaded and while he did not fight at the Battle of Largs, we have already heard that his uncle Ruari fought fiercely there for Haakon. Haakon's defeat, therefore, brought some embarrassment for the clan. The Treaty of Perth in 1266 saw the Norse superiority over the Isles passing to the King of Scots. Alexander III was a true statesman, however, and didn't exact any harsh retribution on the clan for their part in the Battle of Largs. Alexander's death in 1286 saw the loss of one of Scotland's wisest kings and ushered in some dark and troubled times. By 1290, when the Maid of Norway died in Orkney, the Wars of Succession, and of Independence, seemed unavoidable. Angus consistently supported the elder Robert Bruce's claim to the throne until his death in 1300.

Angus's son, Alistair Og, took a different view and upon his accession in 1300, threw all of his weight and influence behind Edward I of England. This was partly due to his recent marriage to a daughter of the family of Lorn and through them, to English interests. In 1308, however, while in arms against King Robert the Bruce in Galloway, he was taken prisoner by Edward Bruce. He died shortly after as a prisoner in Dundonald Castle in Ayrshire.

Angus Og succeeded his brother Alistair as Lord of the Isles. This was good news for Bruce, as Angus had been his friend and loyal adherent since the beginning. The other branch of Clann Cholla that brought men to Bruce early in his campaign were the Clan Ruari, the grandchildren of Ruari of Largs. It was, in part, Angus Og and his 5,000 Islesmen that brought victory and fulfilled Bruce's trust at Bannockburn when he said, 'My hope is constant in thee' – a phrase still on Clanranald's arms today. The victory also assured Clan Donald a place in the right wing of the royal army from that day on. All told, my mother found three many-times-over great-great grandfathers at Bannockburn – Robert the Bruce himself, possibly Donald Mackay and Angus Og. Angus died in 1330 and was buried on Iona. John of Islay, Lord of the Isles, succeeded Angus Og, and ruled the vast lands of Clan Donald for 56 years. He married twice, and both of those marriages are of interest to this tale. His first marriage was to Amie MacRuari, in 1337, heiress to all the MacRuari lands.

John's son by Amie, Ranald, was the founder of Clanranald. Tradition also points to Amie as being responsible for the building of Castle Tioram.

This place, more than any other (more even than Dunadd) calls to me. Loch Moidart is steep-sided and its islands are thickly wooded. Out on the horizon are the 'Small Isles'. The strand at Dorlin is the whitest of sand, curving out into a tidal spit, pointing out towards the rocky islet offshore. Atop that islet stands the great strong bulk of Castle Tioram, encircled by a mighty curtain wall through which only one door beckons.

I have spent hours there, listening to the sea, watching the changing sky, and feeling the past all around me. Far below the castle walls, on the western side, is a shingle beach, where, if the veil wears thin, I can hear the creak of galleys riding at

Castle Tioram

anchor and the flap of their sails. Sometimes they can almost be seen.

And if I leave my twenty-first-century cares together with my twenty-first-century clothes on a rock by the water and dive into the loch, then this tears the veil aside altogether. For what difference is there between then and now, when simplified down to arms cleaving through cold, salty waters, skin tingling and heart pounding with the joyful exertion? And so this is my place of places. Here I can sit and watch the sun dropping from the burnished heavens towards a sea of mellow gold and as the world darkens, the castle stands silhouetted against the sky and seems to live again, hiding age and condition under a cover of night.

Tioram became the ancestral home of Clanranald. It is not with Clanranald that we are most interested, however, but rather with the descendants of John's second marriage. This is one of our main points of convergence, because, in 1357, John of Islay married Margaret Stewart, Princess of Scotland and daughter of King Robert II (my maternal ancestral grandmother, as discussed in Chapter Five).

Thus two strands of ancestry interweave and become one.

John and Margaret had seven children, of whom the eldest was Donald, who became known as Donald of Harlaw when he eventually inherited in 1386. The fourth child was named Alexander, but known as Alasdair Carrach of Keppoch, and we will hear more of his daughter later. The sixth child is recorded as Margaret in the Clan Donald papers, but is known as Lady Elizabeth MacDonald of the Isles in the Clan Mackay records.

John of Islay died in 1386 and was buried on Iona.

In the 25th year of Donald's lordship, after almost two decades of peace, he decided to push his claim to the Earldom of Ross. This was denied him and so he marched, with 10,000 men, on Aberdeen. He wasn't unopposed however.

The most powerful clan in the far north, the Mackays, were not best pleased by the prospect of an even stronger Clan

Donald. Angus Dubh Mackay rallied 2,500 men and met Donald in battle at Dingwall. After a fierce engagement they were beaten, and Angus Dubh Mackay was taken prisoner. Donald continued eastward and clashed with the considerable forces of the Earl of Mar at the village of Harlaw. It was here that the clansmen were encouraged with the appeal 'Sons of Conn, remember hardihood in time of strife'.

Mar was defeated, but there were terrible losses on both sides and so Donald chose to withdraw and recover in the safety of his own lands. He then dealt with Angus Dubh Mackay by making him a family member – marrying him to Donald's own sister, Lady Elizabeth of the Isles.

So here we see the final convergence of the families we have been following.

Angus Dubh and the Lady Elizabeth have stories of their own and we will look at these. But for now, the MacHeths, Clann Cholla, the Norse ancestors and the royal line all distil down into the birth of Neil Mackay in Tongue in 1413. Imprisonment awaited him before he had even reached 15 years of age, and, all in all, he was to live in turbulent times.

Table 4 on page 155 describes the people of the various family branches, from Conn of the Hundred Battles (123 AD) up to Lady Elizabeth of the Isles and the birth of her son Neil in 1413.

CHAPTER SIX

Sons and Lovers

As we have heard, Angus Dubh Mackay was married to Lady Elizabeth MacDonald of the Isles in 1412. This was probably at the suggestion of Donald of Harlaw, who was Lord of the Isles and Lady Elizabeth's brother. Lady Elizabeth came north to the Mackay seat at Tongue, bringing along her niece, Mary, for company. This Mary MacDonald was the daughter of Elizabeth's brother, Alasdair Carrach of Keppoch – the first of the Keppoch MacDonell chiefs of Lochaber. Mary was considered to be attractive and good company.

The marriage of Angus Dubh and Lady Elizabeth was a political marriage and it brought Angus Dubh great power. As a result he was soon described as the third most significant man in the kingdom, after Donald of the Isles and Douglas. The match brought him power, but did it bring him pleasure? It appears not, as he seemed to much prefer the company of Mary to that of his wife. In fact, Elizabeth eventually became so jealous that she sent Mary home to her father in Lochaber.

It transpired that Elizabeth's jealously wasn't just the result of a fevered imagination jumping at shadows. The following year, 1413, Elizabeth was first to bear Angus Dubh a son. This was the Neil Mackay of our convergence, born in Tongue and later to be known as Neil of the Bass (or Neil Vass). Just months later, however, Mary, too, bore Angus Dubh a son – Iain Aberach (meaning 'Iain from Lochaber').

In 1427 Angus was summoned to attend the King (James I) in Inverness, as he was charged with freebooting and cattle stealing. He was found guilty and had to give up his son Neil as a hostage for his good behaviour. Neil, aged 14, was imprisoned on the Bass Rock in the Firth of Forth, which is where he got his name.

The years passed and Angus's landholdings grew. He was given considerable lands in Ross by his brother-in-law, Donald of the Isles. These lands were managed by Angus's nephews, Morgan and Neil. They, in turn, were married to two sisters – the daughters of Angus Murray, chief of the Murrays of Rogart. These two nephews were considered of questionable honour in the Highlands for betraying their own brother, Thomas, to the King in return for a reward some years before. Their connection with Angus Murray, therefore, was bound to lead to mischief, as that man had a greedy heart and a major opportunistic streak.

Angus Murray and the nephews waited with unusual patience, until 1433. Then, with Angus Dubh getting old and failing in sight, they judged that the time was right to strike. Angus Murray sent Morgan and Neil to raise the men of Rogart and Easter Ross to attack Tongue.

Angus Dubh heard of the invasion plans and sent for help to his illegitimate son, Iain, in Lochaber. Although he was only 20, Iain Aberach had already carved a name for himself as a brave and fearless warrior and was known throughout the Highlands.

Meanwhile, Angus Murray's army (the Cataich – meaning those from south Sutherland) were marching into Mackay country. On the way they called in on Iver, the Laird of Shinness. He was the third of Angus Murray's sons-in-law, being married to his eldest daughter, and was known as being the greatest warrior in the north of Scotland at that time. He also seems to have had more honour than his brothers-in-law and father-in-

Grace MacDonald (née Sutherland) – born 1851, died 1931

Hugh MacDonald (seated) and William MacDonald, two sons of Hugh and Grace MacDonald

William MacDonald —
born 1891, died 1963

Annie Mackay —
born 1894, died 1966

William MacDonald (seated) and John MacDonald, the King's Piper, sons of Hugh and Grace MacDonald

House at Gruids, Lairg – home of Robert and Margaret Mackay, and where Annie Mackay (second from left) was born

Wedding picture of William MacDonald and Annie Mackay – Tain, 1923 (also pictured are Sadie Richardson and Willie Campbell)

Willie MacDonald with his first car

Hughie and Donnie, brothers of Margaret MacDonald,
at Gruids, Lairg

Willie MacDonald with his piping class

Willie and Annie MacDonald

Margaret MacDonald marries
David Allison, Hunter's Quay,
1950

Margaret Allison (née
MacDonald) – born 1925

House at Tomonie, Banavie, Fort William –
home of David and Margaret Allison and family

Hugh Allison (the author) –
born 1960

law put together. He told Angus Murray that his cause was not a just one and that he would have no part of it.

Undeterred, the Cataich army carried on towards Tongue. They came over the western side of Ben Loyal at a place called Beallach Duag. Angus Dubh had men out scouting the country and they spotted the advancing Cataich. Although now too old and feeble to fight, Angus Dubh was still a fine general and he put his mind to the coming battle.

Iain Aberach had reached Tongue the previous evening and been given command of the Mackay men. They were badly outnumbered, but, balancing this, Angus Dubh had picked his ground well. He had laid an ambush on Druim na coup, where the enemy would be forced into more manageable numbers by a narrow pass. Then, having chosen the killing ground, he retired a safe distance to Craggie to await the outcome of the battle, leaving Iain Aberach as the Mackay captain on the field.

The Cataich came through the pass at dawn, but the Mackays met them there with flights of arrows, and Iain Aberach, fighting like one of the Celtic heroes of old, so inspired his men with his swordsmanship that they fought fiercely, cutting down the Cataich and slaughtering them without mercy. The survivors broke and streamed away eastwards over the flank of Ben Loyal, hotly pursued by the Mackays. The last man was killed at the southern end of Loch Loyal.

At the last, though, what should have been a great victory turned instead to ashes – a tragedy of almost operatic proportions. From the time that the Murrays left Shinness, Iver's wife had turned shrewish. She taunted him with cowardice, and nagged at him continuously. 'Why will you not help my father?' She seemed deaf to his argument that her father was acting dishonourably and that Angus Dubh had always been a good neighbour to them. Finally, unable to bear more taunting and domestic strife, Iver set out to follow his father-in-law's army. He had 30 miles to cover and so arrived too late for the battle. At this same time, old Angus Dubh felt that it was now safe enough for an old man like himself to approach the site of the battle. Everyone else was gone, the Mackays chasing the last of the invaders and bringing them down. Angus Dubh, being nearly blind, was looking among the fallen for the bodies of his nephews. This was when Iver arrived on the scene and, mistaking what he saw for someone robbing the dead, shot an arrow through Angus Dubh's heart. Iver was horrified when he realised his mistake and turned at once for home. He headed back by the same route he had come by, hoping no one would realise who had done the deed. But it was too late – he had already been recognised by some of the Mackay wounded lying on the field.

Lady Elizabeth cried out for vengeance for the death of her husband and Iain Aberach would have been happy to oblige, considering that Angus Dubh was his father. However, there was still some ill feeling from Lady Elizabeth towards Iain, who couldn't help but remind her of her husband's affair with Mary. So she refused Iain. She said that she had the right to choose her own champion. Thus dismissed, Iain Aberach returned home to Lochaber, and it wasn't long after these events that he married the daughter of the chief of the Clan Mackintosh. As time passed, the Lady Elizabeth's desire for revenge was repeatedly frustrated, something which seems only to have sharpened her wish for it. For three years she sent the best men in the country to challenge Iver. Great rewards were promised to anyone who would bring back his head. But no one did. They were all killed, until Iver, tired of this bloodshed, went into hiding.

Finally, finding herself out of options, the Lady Elizabeth sent word to Iain Aberach that if he would bring her Iver's head, she would give him his father's estate, as she was now too old to manage it properly and she was also desperate to avenge the killing of Angus Dubh before her own death. Iain came to Tongue and told the Lady Elizabeth that he would avenge his father's death. But he wasn't interested in the offer of lands. He pointed out that the great estates of the Mackays belonged, by right, to his brother Neil, still a prisoner on the Bass Rock.

Iain now had the difficulty of finding Iver. Shinness was Iver's home place and, of course, the people were happy to help hide him. For some time Iain had no luck and could find no trace of him. Finally he decided to use guile. He waited until all of the local population were occupied in church one Sunday morning. Then he drove the cattle into the corn crop. Iver had been hiding offshore, on Fiag Island in Loch Shin. When he saw the cattle destroying the corn, and no one else available to drive the creatures off, he swam ashore to try to save the crop.

At the end of his swim, as he strode dripping from the loch, Iain was waiting for him and told him to draw his sword. Iver recognised Iain and told him that he would consider it an honour to die at the hands of such a renowned warrior.

Iver was unwilling to draw his sword on Iain. He told Iain that he would let him take his life for the life of his father, whom he had killed by mistake. He understood that Iain must avenge the death of his father, but sought the promise from Iain that he would be fair to the people of Shinness.

'The Story of the Clan Mackay Family' records the encounter between these two warriors: Iver pled, 'I would like you to promise me to be fair to the people of Shinness when you will inherit the estates of your father, and be as good a neighbour to them as he was. Remember I was the only Shinness man among the raiders at Druim na coup.'

Iain replied, 'I know all that and I regret what I have to do. But you know the rules we live by and I could not live with my conscience if I did not revenge the death of the man that sired me.'

'Give it me in the thrapple and make it quick,' said Iver, as he looked Iain unflinchingly in the eyes. Then Iain, with one stroke of his claymore, took off Iver's head.

The next day Iain visited the Lady Elizabeth at Tongue House and Iver's head joined the other table decorations that morning at her breakfast. She was well pleased that at last the murder of

Angus had been avenged and again offered him his father's estates. Iain felt no particular pride in the killing of Iver and courteously refused the offer, wishing only to return home to his wife at Torlundy in Lochaber.

The following year, 1437, Neil was released from the Bass Rock prison. On returning north, he repeated his mother's offer to Iain of his father's lands and leadership of the clan. This time Iain did accept part of the Mackay lands. He settled in the upper part of Strathnaver, stretching from Ben Hee to Achoul on Strathnaver, where his descendants lived for the next 400 years.

These 'Aberach Mackays' were thus the oldest cadet branch of the clan, and took their name from Iain – *Sliochd-ean-Abrich* (progeny of Iain Aberach). They are described as being the most fearless section of the clan and had a reputation for honesty and fair play to their allies – which we shall hear more of in relation to the Battle of Aldicharrish.

I have always been impressed by the virtues and skills ascribed to Iain Aberach, and indeed the Aberach Mackays, and would love to claim direct descent from them. However, in this account we are now going to return to the elder half-brother, and leader of the clan – Neil, the son held hostage in the Bass Rock prison. It's Neil's line we are going to follow, because it's from Neil that my family are descended. To be absolutely accurate, Neil was my 15-times great-grandfather.

Neil married Euphemia Munro (daughter of George Munro of Foulis). Sadly, though, he didn't survive long after leaving the Bass Rock. Records show that he 'ravaged Caithness, soon after his accession', but died later that year, still in his 20s, leaving two sons. These were Angus Roy, born 1440, and John Roy Mackay, who founded another clan branch, the *Sliochd-ean-Roy* (progeny of John Roy).

Angus Mackay, the elder of the two, married a daughter of MacKenzie of Kintail, who bore him a daughter and three sons. His daughter eventually married Alexander Sutherland of

Dilred. Angus helped the Keiths in invading Caithness in 1464, and they won a battle at Blaretannie. He wasn't so lucky some years later – he was burnt to death in the church of Tarbet in 1475 by the men of Ross, with whom he had often clashed.

His three sons were then compelled by the Highland code of honour, which required revenge for the death of a relative. This was thought of as a sacred undertaking. If this vengeance was, for any reason, delayed, then it reflected upon the honour of the clan.

Angus's eldest son, John Riabhaieh applied to John, Earl of Sutherland for help. The Earl sent his uncle, Robert Sutherland, with a company of men. These forces joined the army that John had raised and, with the help of Uilleam (William) Dubh Aberach (son of Iain Aberach), they invaded Strath Oykell, bringing fire and sword to the lands of the Rosses.

The Laird of Balnagown, chief of the Rosses, collected his strength together and attacked the invaders on 11 July 1487 at a place called Aldicharrish. The fighting was long and hard, but the death of Balnagown and 17 of his main followers threw the bulk of the Ross forces into panic and the slaughter continued for the duration of their confused retreat.

This victory came complete with a fair quantity of booty, which the winners divided the same day. The records paint the MacLeods of Assynt as the villains of the piece, as they proposed killing the Sutherlands and taking their share of the plunder. The Earl of Sutherland could, thus, be told that his clansmen had fallen in battle with the Rosses.

The expression 'Ceartas nan Abrich' means 'the justice of the Aberachs' and dates from this time. William Dubh, chief of the Aberach Mackays, refused to listen to the MacLeod proposal and warned Robert Sutherland of the possibility of such treachery, so that he would be ready. Robert, of course, set his men on the defensive and this in itself saved him. The men of Assynt saw that it would be more trouble than the value of the plunder to attack him, so they headed home instead.

Was John Riabhaieh Mackay ever chief of the clan? And what ultimately became of him? I don't know. All I can tell, from both the written records and the oral histories, is that his younger brother, Aodh Roy, became chief very quickly after the Battle of Aldicharrish. Aodh, who had been born in 1460, married the daughter of Norman O'Beolan from Carloway, in Lewis. They had two sons together, that we know of. The eldest was John and the younger was Donald Mackay of Strathnaver, who was born in 1490. Aodh Roy was the first chief of the Mackays to be awarded a royal charter confirming him in his lands. This was significant as it represented the first proper instalment of the clan in their possessions. It was granted by James IV, in 1499, as reward for having caught, on royal warrant, Alexander Sutherland of Dilred.

As we have heard, Sutherland of Dilred was the husband of Aodh's sister. He was, nevertheless, wanted for the murder of an Alexander Dunbar. Aodh, for sake of family honour, sought him out and captured him and ten of his followers. Alexander was sent to the King, who had him tried, condemned and executed, and his lands declared forfeit. Aodh Roy was not only confirmed in his own lands, he was also awarded a substantial portion of Sutherland of Dilred's lands as well.

There were other instances, too, when the Mackays acted in the service of the crown. On several occasions they carried out commissions against other Highland clans. One such campaign was against the outlawed Torquil MacLeod of the Lews. Indeed, Aodh Roy was present at the siege of Stornoway Castle in 1506 when Torquil was captured. In reward, the King gave Mackay yet more land grants in the north and west. Aodh Roy and his brother (probably Neill-Naverigh Mackay) were both at fateful Flodden in 1513, when their King, James IV, fell along with 10,000 other good Scots. They survived the battle. By the time they got home to the north coast, however, they found that the impact of Flodden could be felt in every corner of every land-holding in the country. The rules had altered, the players had changed places and they hadn't seen any of it coming.

CHAPTER SEVEN

The Grudge as an Art Form

ONE OF THE RECURRING THEMES OF THE STEWART DYNASTY was the continuous struggle between monarch and strong and ambitious nobles. Strong Stewart kings could control the situation, but often met with early and untimely ends, leaving infant successors, and so the balance of power would swing away from the throne. Then, when the next monarch took the throne, on coming of age, the reins of government would be firmly (and sometimes savagely) reclaimed by the crown.

The death of James IV at Flodden left the way clear for the most important and influential families to gather yet more strength to themselves. James V was only a year and a half old at the time of his father's death. It would be some years before he was able to exert any control and meantime his titled subjects played politics. They entered into powerful alliances, wrested lands from weaker neighbours and established many interests. Nowhere was this more in evidence than in the north.

The Gordons were one of the most powerful families in the north-east. Indeed the Earl of Huntly was known as the 'Cock of the North'. It therefore signalled grave days ahead for the Mackays when the Earl of Huntly's brother, Adam Gordon of Aboyne, chose to marry Elizabeth, sister and heiress of the 9th

Earl of Sutherland. Up until this time the great families of the north were almost in balance in terms of strength and influence. This match, which combined the might of the Gordons with the existing strength of the Sutherlands, ensured the prominence of the Earls of Sutherland thereafter.

Aodh Roy Mackay was a realist and in 1516 gave his bond of service to Adam, now Earl of Sutherland. Sadly, however, Aodh died later that year and trouble came to the north again. Aodh Roy had two sons, John and Donald. The elder son, John, of course took possession of his father's lands. Unexpectedly, Aodh's brother, Neill-Naverigh, also laid claim to these lands, and backed that up with a plea to the Earl of Caithness to help recover them. Neill was so persistent that the Earl finally gave him the force of men he desired, which he and his two sons then led in the invasion of Strathnaver. They over-ran and defeated John by sheer strength of numbers and he retreated south, with the idea of asking Clan Chattan for help. His brother Donald was therefore left in Strathnaver to defend himself as best he could. He had too few men to attack Neill openly in pitched battle, so he bided his time and surprised the invaders by night, at Dalreavigh in Strathnaver, where his small force slew most of their enemies and both of Neill's sons. John Mackay returned quickly when he heard of Donald's victory and together they drove from Strathnaver all of Neill's followers. Their uncle Neill himself had been abandoned by the Earl of Caithness, so he threw himself on their mercy. He said he only required a small maintenance to keep him from poverty for the rest of his life. But John and Donald, motivated by thoughts of vengeance, ignored both mercy and ties of blood and ordered Neill to be beheaded in their presence by the hands of Claff-na-Gep, his own foster brother.

This clearly shows that these brothers had elevated 'holding a grudge' to an art form. The future looked to be dark and bloody, then, when, later that year, the Earl of Sutherland chose to take Mackay lands, particularly those lands which Aodh Roy received by royal charter from King James IV in 1499. John Mackay waited until 1517, when the Earl of Sutherland had gone south to Edinburgh on business. Then, at the head of a mixed force of allies, he pushed south into Sutherland, past that vast upturned keel of a mountain, Ben Klibreck, burning and spoiling everything as he went.

Ben Klibreck

The Countess of Sutherland had stayed at home and when she heard of the invasion she asked for help from her bastard brother, Alexander Sutherland. He mustered the Sutherland men, but also received help from the chief of the Clan Gunn and John Murray of Aberscors. The armies met and fought at Torran-Dubh, near Rogart in Strathfleet.

Sir Robert Gordon, the Sutherland chronicler who lived in that century, said that this 'was the greatest conflict that has hitherto been foughtin between the inhabitants of these countreyes'. John Mackay commanded men from areas across the north, such as Caithness, Strathnaver, Assynt, the Western Isles and others. The battle was long and terrible, but finally the Mackays were defeated, losing several hundred men. John and Donald escaped, but were chased by their enemies until night fell, stopping the pursuit, and they were able to slip home to the north.

This only heightened John's anger and, blaming John Murray for his defeat, he resolved to attack him next. Of course, Torran-Dubh had drained his strength and manpower, and so he asked his kinsmen to help. These were the Aberach Mackays, and they met the Murrays in battle not far from Torran-Dubh. Unfortunately, the Murrays were victorious again and both Aberach leaders and most of their men were slain.

Furious about this second disaster, John Mackay sent two nephews to attack and burn John Murray's town of Pitfour (or Pitfure) in Strathfleet. But this too ended in disaster, with one nephew and most of the men being killed and the other nephew taken prisoner. John Mackay seemed, at that point, to get the message and he submitted, at least temporarily, to the Earl of Sutherland (on his return from Edinburgh) and offered a bond of service to him in 1518.

Hostilities blew up again in 1521–2, with John Mackay this time persuading the illegitimate Sutherland heir, Alexander, to rise against his own brother-in-law, the Earl of Sutherland. Alexander was soon defeated, again by the military prowess of

John Murray. He was beheaded on the spot and his head was sent to Dunrobin on a spear, which was then placed on top of the great tower. After this, the Earl retired to Aboyne on Deeside, leaving his eldest son, another Alexander, this one Alexander Gordon, in charge of Sutherland. John Mackay thought this would be a good time to catch the Sutherlands unaware and perhaps recapture some Mackay lands. He gathered a force and mounted an attack on the parish of Creich, only to be beaten back by Alexander Gordon. The futility of the repeated defeats of four years earlier seem not to have made an impact and John appeared bent on repeating the process.

He invaded again and was beaten by Alexander at the Grinds; Alexander then took further lands from him as punishment for his recent behaviour. Alexander, angered by these repeated attacks, also decided to take the initiative and entered Strathnaver with an army that looted and burned in the hunt for John. But John wasn't to be found, as, rather predictably, he was again south, in Sutherland, on a major cattle raid at Lairg.

Alexander turned his army and marching south, fell on the Mackays in a surprise attack. It was complete defeat for John and he only just escaped with his life by swimming to the island of Eilean-Minric, near Lairg. He hid there all day and night, returning home the next day. Alexander Gordon, meanwhile, rescued all of the stolen cattle and returned them to their owners. John seems finally to have accepted that throwing his strength against the unassailable Sutherlands was a wasted exercise. He, for a second and last time, gave his bond of service to the Sutherlands in 1522. This brought a relative peace to the north for three decades.

John died in 1529 and was succeeded by his brother. Donald Mackay, who had married Helen Sinclair (a daughter of Alexander Stempster, a son of the 2nd Earl of Caithness), led the Clan until his death in 1550. James V was, by now, adult, and the balance of power was swinging back towards the Crown. One result of this for Donald Mackay was the reinstatement of the bulk of his lands, by the King, in 1539. This was one of the reasons for Donald, and his son Aodh Dubh (born around 1520), loyally following James to the debacle and defeat at Solway Moss in November 1542, where the Scots army broke and was routed by the English.

Aodh Dubh was taken prisoner and sent captive to England. Donald returned to Edinburgh with James V three days after the battle. There the King bestowed upon him, by charter dated 28 November 1542, the forfeited lands of several individuals who wouldn't fight during the battle. A little over two weeks later James was dead (some say of a broken heart) and Scotland was plunged into the minority of Mary, Queen of Scots, another infant Stewart.

Aodh Dubh was back from England by 1550, when he inherited the clan leadership following Donald's death. The first problem he had to deal with was a familiar one – attempted land grabs by the Sutherlands. There were a number of minor conflicts and in 1555 Aodh Dubh was summoned to appear before the Queen Regent at Inverness to answer for attacking John, Earl of Sutherland's lands while the Earl was in France with the Queen Regent herself. Aodh Dubh didn't appear to answer the charges, so a commission was given to Earl John to capture him. Strathnaver was invaded and the Castle of Borve was besieged. When Borve fell, Earl John hanged its captain and then demolished the castle. Aodh Dubh was captured shortly afterwards in 1556 and imprisoned in Edinburgh Castle for some time. A cousin, John Mor Mackay, led the clan during Aodh Dubh's imprisonment. It was John Mor Mackay who invaded Sutherland for the last time. He burnt and looted in Navidale, but was caught and defeated by the Sutherland men at the water of Garbharry in Berriedale. One source states 'this is the last conflict betwixt Sutherland and Strathnaver'. This was only partly true.

On his release from Edinburgh Castle, Aodh Dubh returned north and married Christine, daughter of William Sinclair of

Dun. Before long, Aodh was drawn into the conflicts surrounding the young Mary, Queen of Scots. He was one of those who attacked and slew Huntly at the Battle of Corrichy in 1562, after the Gordon plottings came to light. This raised the fortunes of the Mackays again, as Aodh Dubh attended Queen Mary when she visited Inverness later that year. She granted him remission for all previous crimes, and royal favour for his actions against the disgraced Gordons and Sutherlands. This favour was temporary, however, and completely reversed by 1565, when Mary became reconciled with the new Earl of Huntly. The Gordons were again top dogs and in 1566 one of Mary's first gifts to the newly favoured Huntly consisted of a grant of the Mackay lands. Unable to take possession, Huntly was happy to sell the lands back to Aodh, but he did retain the feudal superiority, which he granted to the Earl of Sutherland.

Aodh Dubh went warring into Sutherland only once more before his death in what really was probably the last active conflict between the two houses. Alexander, Earl of Sutherland, was a minor in the care of Huntly in Grampian in 1570. The Earl of Caithness therefore felt that the time was right to settle an old score that he had with the Murrays of Dornoch. He therefore sent his son, John, accompanied by Aodh Dubh, to deal with the Murrays. They burnt the town and the cathedral, but still the Murrays held out, beseiged in the castle. Finally, after a month they surrendered and retreated to Huntly, until Alexander came into his inheritance as Earl.

Aodh Dubh returned home to Strathnaver, where he died the next year, 1572. His eldest son by Christine Sinclair seems to have died before him. That son would have borne the title 'of Strathnaver'. It was his second son, therefore, that inherited the clan leadership and being the second son he bore the title 'of Farr'. This was Uisdean Dubh Mackay of Farr, born 1561.

Uisdean (called Hugh in the English records) was a minor when his father died and thus spent his early years as a ward of the Earl of Caithness. In Calder's *History of Caithness*, he is described as 'a most unprincipled man of the two crimes of the deepest dye – murder and adultery'.

Strong words, but deserved, if the tale of 'the woman of Lone' is true. Although, if it is true, then I don't quite understand why Hugh Mackay seems to have gone unpunished.

In his youth, Hugh Mackay was deer hunting in north-west Sutherland. He happened to meet the woman who lived at Lone, near Achfary, was immediately taken with her beauty and asked her to be his mistress. She rebuffed him, answering that she was a married woman and would be no man's mistress as long as her husband was alive. Hugh Mackay left the house, but shortly thereafter met with the man of Lone, and beheaded him with an axe. This earned him the sobriquet Uisdean Dubh na tuath (Black Hugh of the axe). He returned to the house, where the petrified woman surrendered to his wants.

Nine months later she bore him a son, who was named Donald Balloch, due to an axe-shaped birthmark on his neck. ('Ball' is Gaelic for 'axe'.) This Donald was fostered by the Morrisons of Kinlochbervie.

Hugh Mackay was twice married. The first marriage, to Lady Elizabeth Sinclair, second daughter of the fourth Earl of Caithness, seems not to have created much stir. They had one daughter. The second marriage was to Lady Jane Gordon, the elder daughter of the 11th Earl of Sutherland. It was before this wedding that Hugh arranged for a man called Donald MacLeod, who was at that time outlawed from his own clan, to marry his mistress, the woman of Lone, in order to permanently wipe that episode from his past. He also gave them the Davoch of Hope, where they settled at a place called Achlochie.

And what of Donald Balloch?

He grew to become a famous warrior among the Morrisons, and with a company of Morrison mercenaries, took service with the Earl of Caithness. The closing years of the century saw war between the earls of Caithness and of Sutherland. Ironically,

Hugh Mackay found himself supporting his father-in-law, the Earl of Sutherland, in this conflict, which put him on the opposite side from Donald Balloch. There were a number of occasions when Donald inflicted substantial defeats on his father's forces.

They were finally brought together in peace, however. The outlaw, Donald MacLeod, had persuaded Donald Balloch to join in on an ill-starred attack on the Scourie MacLeods. The attack went well enough and they seized the village. Things began to look bad, however, when the Laird of Assynt (the proprietor of Scourie) arrived with an army to attack the Morrisons. Then, to complete the party, Hugh Mackay arrived with 500 men and avoided further bloodshed by buying Scourie from the Laird of Assynt. He then gave the lands of Scourie to his son, Donald Balloch.

The times that we have been describing since Aodh Roy's death in 1516 were arguably amongst the most savage in the Mackay clan history. This was probably due to the fact that their successive chiefs throughout the sixteenth century were under such pressure just to retain their freedom in the face of overwhelming and continuous force from the Sutherlands.

It was a turbulent century at large in the country too and yet, oddly, it was also a time for the expansion of learning in Scotland. Although St Andrews and Glasgow both had universities dating from the fifteenth century, it was in the sixteenth that Edinburgh got its first and Aberdeen its second. In 1593, James VI added to this educational development by replacing most books, previously used, with new editions.

Hugh Mackay continued to lead the clan for many more years. He lived through the Union of the Crowns of Scotland and England in 1603, when James VI of Scotland became known as James I of Britain as well.

Hugh and Lady Jane had many children, of whom I shall mention three. One of their many girls, Mary, born in 1585, is one of our direct forebears, as we shall see. Their eldest son,

Donald, was born in 1591 and became the first Lord Reay. The second son, born about 1595, known as John Mackay of Strathy, is another direct forebear. Hugh Mackay died in 1614, leaving Clan Mackay considerably more settled and prosperous than he had found it.

CHAPTER EIGHT

Hardmen and Healers

DONALD MACKAY LED THE CLAN MACKAY FROM THE TIME OF his father's death in 1614. It was a period of particular upheaval across Europe and Donald was to achieve military fame across the continent during the next 15 years. We will hear more of this as the century unfolds.

Meanwhile, Donald's sister Mary had married Hector Munro of Coul in 1611 and later the couple received Eriboll as Mary's share of the Mackay estate. Although Hector owned Coul and Pittentrail, near Rogart, they came to live in Eriboll, and took a lot of people with them. These were in-laws and relatives of the Munros and so for the first time surnames like Douglas, Ross and MacDonald appear in the Mackay country.

These particular MacDonalds will be significant to our story two centuries downstream, so it is worth taking time out to consider who they were, and where they came from. The oral tradition outlines clearly that they were descended from Alasdair Carrach, of whom we first heard in 'The Convergence', described as the fourth child of John, Lord of the Isles and Margaret, Princess of Scotland.

Angus of Fersit was Alasdair Carrach's only son and the tradition states that the Melness MacDonalds are descended from Angus. My grandfather always stated that he was of the Clanranald MacDonalds and indeed the Keppoch branch are known as the Clanranalds of Lochaber. My mother was also told by Hugh MacDonald (of Skinnet) that his grandmother passed him the same oral genealogy as she had learnt from her forebears.

Angus of Fersit married a daughter of MacPhee of Glen Pean and their younger son, Alasdair nan Gleann, became 5th Keppoch chief. He died in 1498 and was succeeded by his son, Donald Glas, who had married a daughter of Cameron of Lochiel. Donald Glas entered into a bond of mutual security with Munro of Foulis early in the sixteenth century and so a number of MacDonalds went north to Foulis, and later to Rogart with a Munro sub-chief. The final migration, as we have heard, was in the mid-seventeenth century, to Durness, with Hector Munro after he had married Mary Mackay.

Mary's younger brother, John of Strathy, married Agnes Sinclair of Murkle in 1618, four years after his elder brother, Donald, had become clan chief. So from what particular family did Agnes spring before she consented to become one of our ancestral grandmothers? Her father, James Sinclair of Murkle, was a grandson of the Earl of Caithness. Her mother, Elizabeth, was a daughter of Robert Stewart, Earl of Orkney. Most families have the odd maverick lurking in the historical cupboard. It's just unfortunate that my mother's family comes complete with dark-hearted monsters instead of skeletons, in the closet. And these monsters were Robert Stewart and his son Patrick Stewart, known as the Wicked Earls of Orkney!

Earl Robert of Orkney was born in 1533, an illegitimate son of James V and Euphemia Elphinstone (and therefore a half-brother of both Mary, Queen of Scots and James, Earl of Moray). He was given the episcopal lands and revenues of the Northern Isles in 1568 and he ruled his domain with a will of iron. Peter Anderson states of Robert, in his book *Robert Stewart*: 'His contemporaries variously describe him as arrogant, obsequious, evil, dissolute, treacherous. These accusations are nowhere disputed, nor are compensating virtues (if any could so compensate) set to his account.' He was succeeded by his son, Earl Patrick, and altogether the Northern Isles laboured under the tyranny of these earls for almost 50 years. Their reign was characterised by a cruelty and brutality that was extreme even for the time.

Earl Patrick was 28 when he came to power on the death of his father. His rule was even more dark and vicious than that of Earl Robert and earned him the nickname 'Black Patie'. However, as well as his harsh oppression of the local population, he was also known for his arrogance and greed, and the extravagances that his wealth could finance. Earl Patrick's affluent lifestyle is described in the *Historie and Life of King James the Sext*, where it says:

> His pomp was so great, as he never went from his castle to the kirk, nor abroad otherwise, without the convoy of 50 musketeers and other gentlemen of convoy and guard . . . He also had his ships directed to sea to intercept pirates and collect tribute of foreign fishers that came yearly to these seas. Whereby he made sic [such] collection of great guns and other weapons of war, as no house, palace, nor castle, yea in all of Scotland were not furnished with the like.

Earl Patrick's love of finery expressed itself in his building projects. He constructed Scalloway Castle in Shetland and remodelled his father's palace at Birsay. His most ambitious project was the building of the Earl's Palace in Kirkwall, combined with a sympathetic alteration to the neighbouring Bishop's Palace. These works are a mastery in beauty and spacious style; they hint at a ruler completely at ease with himself and lacking the slightest guilt concerning the lives that were ground under to provide the building funds.

In fact, these exorbitant works were to be his undoing. By 1606 he was heavily in debt and ignored a summons from the

Privy Council to explain complaints about his extremely tyrannical rule. Bishop James Law, appointed in 1607, was determined to put a stop to the oppression suffered by the people of Orkney. The Bishop, a close friend of King James, presented the King with a petition describing conditions in Orkney. In 1610, Earl Patrick was indicted on seven charges of treason and imprisoned in Edinburgh Castle. An extract of his trial records:

> The said Earl, leaving no sort of extraordinary oppression and treasonable violence unpractised against the said inhabitants of Orkney and Shetland [. . .] has compelled the most part of them to work to him in all manner of work and labour by sea and land [. . .] and all other sorts of servile and painful labour, without either meat, drink, or hire.

The Earl's illegitimate son — named Robert, after his grandfather — rose in rebellion during his father's imprisonment. By way of justification, he said he was following his father's instructions to retake the family's possessions and collect rents. This was supposedly in readiness for his father's anticipated release.

Earl George Sinclair of Caithness was given royal commission to oppose this rebellion, and he led, and paid for, an expedition to Orkney. There was a long siege of Kirkwall Castle and the Bishop's Palace, during which heavy cannon had to be used. Robert Stewart was ultimately betrayed by one of his own men and captured. He was convicted of treason and hanged in January 1615.

Patrick Stewart, Orkney's most hated noble, was also found guilty of treason in 1615, and was beheaded. The final astonishing episode in the life of this wicked earl is that his beheading had to be postponed for several days to give him time to learn the Lord's Prayer. Earl Patrick (Black Patie) had been dead for three years at the time that his niece, Agnes, married John of Strathy in 1618.

Donald Mackay, the leader of the clan, had become Sir Donald Mackay of Farr. He had spent this same time period learning about estate management and buying yet more landholdings for the Mackays. As chief, Donald had two main preoccupations. Firstly, how was he to improve his financial status? Secondly, how could he go about keeping significant numbers of unruly younger sons busy and out of trouble? The religious turmoil across the continent gave him adequate opportunity to do both. In 1626, he raised a regiment to fight on the side of the Protestant forces in the Thirty Years War. It was during these campaigns that he acquired a reputation as a skilled and brave commander.

Donald Mackay's timing in choosing when to apply for a warrant to raise troops for the German service couldn't have been better. The Crown was bound to sanction such an endeavour, as Charles I's sister was the wife of one of the principal Protestant princes of Germany (the Elector Palatine and King of Bohemia). It was these princes to whose aid Donald was sailing.

Mackay's regiment was, in the main, recruited from Sutherland. The initial force of 3,000 men were largely found from Donald's own lands and the officers were nearly all younger sons from the 'landed' houses of the north. They included Mackays, Sinclairs and Munros, amongst others. In fact, the main chronicler of the regiment, including its history and successes, was an officer called Monroe. He wrote one of the earliest printed British military records – a book published in 1637, entitled *Monroe's Expedition*.

The regiment embarked for Germany in 1626 and Donald joined them in Holstein in early 1627. They were in the service of the King of Denmark and it's reported that, while on the continent, the defence of the Pass of Oldenberg was one of their finest feats. It was due to such military engagements that they soon became known as the 'Invincible Scots'.

Ironically, the same ferocity and dedication that made their name also reduced their numbers quite dramatically. For this reason Donald had to return home to Scotland the following year, to renew his regiment by some further recruiting. News of his exploits in Holstein had reached home and, as a result, King Charles raised him to the peerage by bestowing on him the title 'Lord Reay'. This reward came in February 1628.

The Mackay regiment was released from its service with Denmark on the occasion of the declaration of peace in 1629. But still Donald, Lord Reay, didn't lead the men home. Instead, he signed up with Gustavus Adolphus of Sweden. In 1630, Gustavus began the campaign that was to make him known as the 'Liberator of Germany' and the Mackay regiment quickly became a favourite cadre of his.

Over the course of the next eight months, history would have us believe that Gustavus successfully captured over 80 German cities and castles and in all of these actions Donald's corps were actively involved.

Again, after about a year there came a need for yet more recruits and Lord Reay returned home to find them. All told, he recruited about 10,000 men over the whole period, for the wars. However, this time when he sent out the fresh force, he didn't join them, instead becoming entangled with politics at home and losing royal support. His difficulties took both time and money to fix. By the time he could go to join the regiment it was too late. He had lost his initial investment and Gustavus had died unexpectedly in Lutzen in 1632. Any hope of financial reimbursement went with Gustavus and so Lord Reay returned home, a poorer man, to Strathnaver.

His royalty-related problems seem not to have dimmed his enthusiasm for the monarchy, however, and when Charles I began facing the problems of the Presbyterian Revolution, and the Solemn League and Covenant, Lord Reay gave him much help and support. He even went to Denmark in 1643 to raise ships, arms and money for the King. On his return he was seized at Newcastle, imprisoned at Edinburgh and only released after the Battle of Kilsyth. Although he again immediately joined the

King, he sadly became a political sacrifice — the Covenanters requiring King Charles to exempt him from any future royal pardons. He left Scotland in 1648 to settle in Denmark. There he became famous as the main founder of the Scots mercenary service abroad. Life didn't treat him well, though, and by the following February he was dead. His remains were brought home and buried in Strathnaver. One of the eulogies had him as: 'A man of quick wit, speedy resolution and diversible qualities'.

What amazes me most is that during this very busy and military life, Donald, Lord Reay, married five times and left so many children.

During the time of these wars, Donald's younger brother, John of Strathy, had a son, in 1625, known as John of Skerray. And in 1630 Donald's elder sister, Mary of Eriboll, had a daughter called Margaret Munro. These two, first cousins, were married, and in 1660 they had a son, whom they named Hector Mackay. Hector was born at the end of Cromwell's rule. The Mackays, as we have heard, were supporters of the King and are reputed to have fought at the Battle of Worcester in 1651 at the side of King Charles II. The monarchy was restored in 1660 — the year of Hector's birth — and Charles II was proclaimed King.

The Gaelic for Hector is 'Eachin', and so after his family went to Durness they were known as belonging to 'Eachin Skerray'. Because of this, in the old parish registers of Durness, his descendants can be traced very easily.

Hector married Margaret Mackay of Borley (and as an aside, I can tell you that she was the great-granddaughter of Donald Balloch, of whom we heard earlier). Hector and Margaret had four sons, the eldest of whom was Donald Mackay of Skerray and the youngest John of Musal. We'll hear much more about Donald shortly, as it is through him that our line runs. But first a bit about young John of Musal, who was born about 1700. By the early 1720s he was manager of both the cattle and the deer hunts, but not the fishings in Strathmore. He took into his household a herd boy, Robert Mackay, or Rob Donn (pronounced Down) – of whom we shall hear a great deal more, in Chapter Nine. John married Catherine Beaton, who was a direct descendant of the great healer, Fearchar Beaton, and the Beatons that came from Ireland in the fourteenth century. Although one step to the side of the main family line, it is worth looking more closely at Catherine's family, as they were such an exceptional phenomenon.

It is said that when Angus Og, Lord of the Isles, married Agnes of Connacht, she came to the Western Highlands complete with 140 men as a dowry. They represented 24 different families and among these was the medical dynasty known first as the MacBeths and later as the Beatons.

There were some schools scattered throughout Scotland in the fourteenth century. In fact, it was Malcolm Canmore's Queen, Margaret, who began the process of having a school in every parish, under the authority of the Church. In the clan system, however, learning and training tended to be dynastic. Each clan had their own bard (poet and writer) seanachaidh, pipers and also their own doctor and teacher. These specialised areas attracted particular families and hence the Beatons were physicians, with at least 19 branches of the family practising to different clans across the Highlands and Islands.

These medical men (and it was at that time a wholly male preserve), also enjoyed national recognition and royal patronage. Robert the Bruce's chief of medicine was Patrick MacBeth and Patrick's son Gilbert was physician to David II. It is further rumoured that every Scottish monarch from then until James IV had a Beaton as a doctor.

The Lords of the Isles describes the Beatons as follows:

> They followed the teachings of Avicenna the Persian [. . .] the basis of European practice for over 500 years. [. . .] The Beatons possessed a Gaelic copy of Avicenna's eleventh-

century work long before translation into English, or faculties
of medicine were established in universities of Scotland and
England.

So, which of the many Beaton branches did Catherine come
from? Pleasingly there are some references to names we have
already heard in our tales. A royal charter by Robert II and his
son Alexander, Wolf of Badenoch, in 1379, confirms a grant of
lands of Melness and Hope to '*Ffercado medico nostro*'
(Fearchar, our physician). Descendants of Fearchar Beaton gave
these lands back to the chief of Mackay in 1511, when they
moved south. They went to Easter Ross, where by a curious
twist of fate they became hereditary healers to the Munros of
Foulis. Now, as we have already heard, a number of Munro's
people followed a sub-chief to Rogart to become the Munros of
Coul. Then, in the mid-seventeenth century, many followed
Hector Munro of Coul to the north coast when his wife, Mary,
came into her inheritance. And thus Catherine Beaton, direct
descendant of Fearchar, found herself back in the lands that
the Beatons had left 200 years earlier. She married John of
Musal (youngest brother of Donald Mackay of Skerray) and
together they lived in Strathmore.

Donald had been born in Skerray around 1690 and would
therefore have been about two years old at the time of the
Massacre of Glencoe in 1692. This was in the reign of King
William II and III, who, it is said, gave the go-ahead for the
extermination of the MacDonalds of Glencoe. A little bit like
some of today's world leaders, he introduced the 'deniability
factor'. By getting the Master of Stair to sign the offending
document he could later deny any knowledge of the action. I
think nowadays they call it 'Black Ops'.

Donald would have been about 17 at the time of the Union of
the Parliaments in 1707. Around the time of the 1715 Jacobite
Rising, Donald married Esther Gunn, daughter of Donald Gunn,
chief of the Clan Gunn. They had a large family, but we only

know the names of two of them. Hector, the eldest, was born in Skerray in 1720, and his younger brother was called John (sometimes, for reasons we'll hear later, he was called 'John who found the gold').

The people described in chapters Six, Seven and Eight are illustrated by Table 5, page 156.

CHAPTER NINE

Words on the Wind

DONALD MACKAY LIVED ALL HIS LIFE ON THE NORTH COAST, and so did generations of his descendants. In 1723, three years after the birth of Hector, Donald sold his tack of Skerray to Lord Reay, and went to live in Island Chaorie in the parish of Durness. And after this he moved to Achunlochie (still in the parish of Durness). He and his descendants lived there until his great-grandson (also called Donald) was evicted in the early nineteenth century, so were obviously there at the time of the 1745 Jacobite Rising.

This Rising was the dynastic struggle between the House of Stewart and the House of Hanover. It was also when the last battle on British soil took place – the Battle of Culloden Moor in 1746. The Jacobite forces were led by Bonnie Prince Charlie, while the Government troops were led by his cousin, the Duke of Cumberland (known ever after as 'Butcher Cumberland'). The Jacobites suffered a final and crushing defeat. The aftermath of the battle was terrible and widespread atrocities took place throughout the Highlands in the weeks immediately following the battle.

The Mackay clan had been involved in the conflict, but on the Government side, something that W. F. Skene bitterly criticised them for in his book *The Highlanders of Scotland*. However, loyalties and motivations were far from clear-cut in this civil war.

The earlier support and loyalty that the Mackays had shown to the Stewart dynasty had gone largely unrewarded and was a major factor in the financial problems which beset the 1st Lord Reay. The 3rd Lord Reay, George, had avoided further financial ruin by supporting the Government in the Jacobite Risings of 1688 and 1715. His main worry was still the prospect of land disputes with the house of Sutherland. To secure his position, then, he signed an agreement with the Earl of Sutherland, just prior to Prince Charles Edward Stuart's arrival at Glen Finnan. The agreement read: 'To secure our acting with mutual harmony and uniting the strength of both our families [. . .] for securing the present happy establishment in Church and State and for defeating the designs of his Majesty's enemies'. In this way, George, 3rd Lord Reay, protected his people from the miseries, punishments and land seizures that followed each of the Jacobite Risings.

Donald would have been 55 at the time of the conflict, and Hector 25. As yet, no record has been found which chronicles precisely their activities in the 1745 Rising. It is likely, however, that they mustered with the rest of the clan in October and served with either the Earl of Sutherland's or Lord Loudoun's regiment.

At the request of Scottish Lord President Duncan Forbes of Culloden, the second muster of Mackays served mainly in Lord Loudoun's regiment, guarding Inverness and a number of other key locations in the north. It was also Loudoun's forces which surprised and captured Lord Lovat at Castle Dounie in early December.

The following spring brought great excitement to the Mackay country. The British naval ship *Sheerness* pursued an armed Jacobite sloop in a furious sea-battle, along the north coast. This vessel, the *Prince Charles,* was originally called the *Hazard*. She carried the pay-chests of the Jacobite army, £13,000 in French gold, and was also receiving the worst in this long-running engagement. That was when her captain, in an effort to escape, made an error of monumental proportions. He veered into the Kyle of Tongue, a Hanoverian centre of power, and there he ran aground on the shoals, south of Rabbit Island.

Lord Reay watched from his windows, as the *Sheerness* stood offshore, pouring fire into the stricken craft. The French and Spanish soldiery and the crew fled the ship and, taking the gold, this motley force of 120 men headed south.

They reached the end of the Kyle and headed past Ribigill Farm, but before they slipped away over the shoulder of Ben Loyal, they were intercepted by local troops – both Sheriff's men and a detachment of Lord Loudoun's. That magnificent horseshoe of mountains known as Kintail Mackay echoed to the sound of gunfire and when all was quiet again some of the Spaniards lay dead and the rest of the Jacobites were prisoners. One of the pay-chests was broken and another was lost. Enter John 'who found the gold'!

This was Hector's younger brother, who found a bag of *Louis d'or* (French gold) jettisoned by the fleeing sailors after the *Prince Charles* came to grief near Melness. John took this gold to Lord Reay, with the intention of buying Ribigill Farm with it. (Ribigill Farm was famed for rich lands and fertility.) However, not unsurprisingly, Lord Reay claimed that the gold belonged to the Hanoverian king, George II. He took the gold from John, but didn't sell him Ribigill Farm. It isn't known what Lord Reay did with the gold thereafter. The story followed John's grandson to Melness and it helps to identify the family in the records (John who found the gold was an ancestor of Hugh MacDonald of Skinnet).

My ancestor, Hector of Achunlochie, had trained as a drover, as many tacksmen (landholders) were at that time encouraging their sons to learn extra skills or trades. The tack was the piece of land which a man would hold from his chief in return for service. But the old systems were ending, and

skills and trades were good insurance for anyone in danger of
emigration. Hector's eldest son, John Mackay of Achunlochie,
was born in Durness, about 1756. John was a cooper by trade,
and married Barbara Mackay (of the Skerray Mackays) with
whom he had a large family. One of his sons (my great-great-
great-grandfather) was Donald, who suffered eviction from
Achunlochie. He married Jean Mackay, who was in turn the
granddaughter of Rob Donn, of whom we have already heard
a whisper. We'll return to Donald and Jean later, but for now
we need to consider the land, and the life, of Rob Donn.

Ben Loyal

Then, as now, all along the north coast, from Cape Wrath to
Dunnet Head, the land stands hard against the northern seas. A
series of blunt headlands refute the surging crash of the waves.

Inland, there runs a cross-stitch of valleys and upland grazings, each separated from the next by the high places. The lonely sentinels of Arkle and Foinaven and the giants we heard of earlier (Ben Hope and Ben Loyal) all serve to hold apart those softer, gentler glens and straths where the people have made their homes. And everything changes, by the day and by the season. On a day when the sun shines down, the full range of mountain, moor and strath blazes in a display of scent and colour. On a day when the Atlantic gales sweep in, everything turns shades of blue-black slate and the rain pulses across the land, like a heavy, secretive curtain. But during those evenings when the skies are clear and luminous and the moon rides high and white on a light-blue canvas, then the scene is incomparable, almost mythic. Possibilities dance and shimmer on the far horizon and, underfoot, something seems almost ready to waken.

The power in the land sleeps most lightly in the far north. The landscapes are deep and old. The rock foundations of the West Moine are amongst the oldest known, and in places where the soil is thin, the bones of the world show through, upthrust against the sky.

Norse myth and Celtic legend intermingle here in pools amid the heather – groundwater from which the wellsprings of creativity flow. And if you listen very carefully, just when the northern light is at its most luminous and when the wind is blowing through Strathmore, you may like to think that you hear words on the wind. Words inspired by this remarkable place and by the remarkable and hardy people who live here. And without doubt, the words that resonate most powerfully are those of Robert Mackay, known as Rob Donn.

Rob Donn somehow functioned perfectly as both an illiterate northern clansman and one of the greatest of Scotland's bards/poets. He was born in the white and stormy winter of 1714 into 1715, first drawing breath at Allt na Caillich in Strathmore, that valley to the west of Ben Hope.

It was the same year as George I came to the throne. And George was also the name of the 3rd Lord Reay, chief from 1680–1748. Lord Reay was well thought of by his people, who called him *Am Morair Mor* (the Great Lord). He had four sons and when Hugh, the second son, was old enough to marry the heiress of Bighouse, he was first sent to John of Musal to serve an apprenticeship in estate management.

Farther up the strath, Rob Donn's mother was well known as a reciter of Ossianic tales and had given her son a good grounding in the legendary landscape. From the first, though, Rob Donn's words were about the stepping-stones of human life and people's doings. His earliest alleged stanza was at the age of three – a reproach against the buttons on his short frock for being round the back and so making him inadequate in the tying of them.

John of Musal came to hear of the young lad from Allt na Caillich who had been composing such verses since his earliest years, and thus he invited this seven year old into his house as a herd boy. And so Rob Donn came to Musal and the long-house became home to him as well as to John, his wife Catherine and Hugh of Bighouse.

Much of the traditional long-house was taken up with a byre for the livestock and the rest was often divided into four rooms: the chamber (which was a living-room/guest room); children's sleeping room; parents' sleeping room; and the longest room – the servants' hall. This servants' hall (or *'cearn'* in Gaelic) was where Rob Donn sat among the servants, separated from the byre by a slim partition. Here he wrote one of his earlier works, in revolt against the chores expected of him and about the short-temperedness of Catherine, the mistress of the house. This poem is the first of those which I've included in the Bard's Appendix at the end of this book.

As Rob Donn grew to adulthood, his joys were twofold: firstly, taking part in the great deer hunts in the Reay Forest;

secondly, the experience of cattle-droving. Some of these droves took him as far away as the cattle-fair at Crieff, in the company of John, and Hugh of Bighouse. There he was introduced to a wider society than that of Mackay country, and began formulating his own incisive views on the motivations and pressures which cause people to react as they do.

The other inevitable outcome of both his travel and new maturity was an interest in the opposite sex. His verses lead us to believe that he was popular with women. This seems likely, as his poetry is filled with a surprising understanding of how the world looked through their windows. He also spoke with a vigour, and sometimes a sensuality, that would have attracted interest.

What he didn't have, however, was social standing. And while that didn't hold him back in romantic liaisons of no importance (one-night stands?) it was an unclimbable mountain when he fell in love and asked Ann Morrison to marry him. She refused, throwing him over in favour of marriage to a carpenter. Rob Donn's response was predictable – he set the episode to words that still have feeling and relevance today. It is worth reflecting, though, that each of his works is considerably more subtle in the original Gaelic. These verses have a shine, even in English, but in the tongue in which they were composed, they are like quicksilver seen through fine crystal. Translation into English leads to the loss of many shadings of meanings. These include the fact that the word for a carpenter also means 'free', and that '*Air mo chinn*' can mean 'behind my croft', but it also means 'awaiting me'. The end result – '*Is trom leam an airidh*' (The Shieling is a Sad Place for Me) – is generally considered one of Scotland's finest love songs, and it is included as the second work in the Appendix.

Almost as an aside, Rob Donn throws in the extra barb about six other men showing interest in Ann. While this doesn't seem too forward, we should perhaps not lose sight of the fact that he composed another, simpler, lampoon which set riddles as to whom these six might be. All of this, though, is delivered in the particular satire common, even today, in the far north west, and Ann Morrison seemed not overly upset by the unexpected spotlight. Rob Donn wasn't a man to mope or fret over Ann's rejection. Before long he was courting Janet Mackay, with much more success, and after they were married in about 1734, they moved to Bad na h-achlais, near Loch Hope. The marriage was lasting and happy, and Janet is described as having a ready wit, an amiable disposition and a good singing voice. The two of them often entertained at ceilidhs throughout the north.

The Reformed Christian religion of the Calvinists was a very significant influence on Rob Donn's life and upon his bardic development. But it couldn't be called overwhelming. As observed in Ian Grimble's book *The World of Rob Donn,* he never permitted the Calvinist doctrine of justification by faith alone to undermine his belief in the saving power of good works. And although he was sometimes known to moralise, his theme was Man, not God. That notwithstanding, he did identify the Reverend Murdo MacDonald as the most important influence on his life. One outcome of his association with Reverend MacDonald was his love of music and with that came the significant body of composition of original Gaelic airs, which amounted to more than any other Gaelic poet of his century.

So who were his contemporaries at that time?

The hereditary bards of the Gaelic world were the MacMhuirichs, who were part of a literary lineage with close and scholarly links to the libraries of Ireland. Donald MacMhuirich of South Uist would have been the bard in Rob Donn's time, although it isn't thought that they ever met.

Duncan Ban Macintyre, born in 1724, was a poet in praise of nature. His works were rich and descriptive, but dealt with plants and animals, rather than the people who inhabited Rob Donn's lines. Tradition has it that the two men (both illiterate) met on at least one droving expedition and enjoyed each other's words and company.

The other famed Gaelic poet of this time was Alasdair Mac Mhaighstir Alasdair, of the MacDonalds. He was perhaps 20 years older than Rob Donn, fully literate and bilingual. He became the best known of the Jacobite poets, which is unsurprising given the loyalties of the MacDonald clan in the 1745 Rising. Although the Mackays were, as a clan, to be counted as Hanoverian, there were many individuals who fought for the Jacobites.

Rob Donn was one of those with Jacobite sympathies and, following the Jacobite disaster at Culloden, he composed a poem courageously condemning the Government acts of proscription, and in support of Prince Charles Edward Stuart, entreating that he return to Scotland. This poem is included as work three in the Appendix.

Rob Donn was called to trial at Tongue for this 'treasonable' composition, but with his usual quick wit he composed the last two stanzas while en route to trial. His defence was that it was ill-wishers that had repeated his poem without its last two verses, making it appear pro-Jacobite, while if it was heard in its entirety, the court might see otherwise. Amazingly this ruse seemed to work, and the charges were dropped. These last two verses are included in Poem Three.

The contemporary poet whose work was most similar to Rob Donn's was not even a Scot, far less a Gael. He was an Englishman – Alexander Pope. Possibly Pope's best-known work, 'The Rape of the Lock', was composed the year Rob Donn was born. He often said 'the proper study of mankind is man', and both he and Rob Donn lived up to this. They disliked pretension, had an eye for the ridiculous and gave out the lean, mean delivery of the expert satirist.

In 1747, a year after Culloden, John of Musal's daughter Isobel was married. Although she was a childhood friend of Rob Donn's, her mother, Catherine, somehow 'forgot' to add his name to the list of guests. This was perhaps unwise in the extreme and indeed he turned up anyway, complete with a bawdy satire that he'd made up on the way. This is Poem Four in the Appendix. It pokes gentle fun at many wedding guests and is only harsh in the verse concerning Catherine and her father. John who found the gold also makes an appearance, and in the final verse is a suggestion that it was the bridegroom himself that stole the missing trousers.

As he grew older, Rob Donn's attentions became deeper in terms of subject matter and he composed a large body of verse known as *The Elegies*. Many people consider that his best works may be numbered amongst these. George, 3rd Lord Reay, died in 1748, and was commemorated in this way. He was succeeded by his son Donald, who became 4th Lord Reay.

At about this same time, Rob Donn began to be viewed as something of a folk hero, particularly with regard to the issue of the rights of the common man to hunt deer. He stood up fiercely for the view that forbidding 'the taking of a deer' was an assumption of power totally unprecedented and unwarrantable on the part of their superiors.

He proposed the saying *'Is ionraic a' mheirle na feidh'* (Righteous theft is the killing of deer). This challenged the gentry far more seriously than his Jacobite leanings, and he was temporarily exiled to Fresgill, on the Moine. Even today folks from the Highlands are often heard to ask: 'Where is the law and the logic when, if you take a deer by hunting, it belongs to the estate and you're guilty of poaching, but if your car hits a deer and is written off, then that deer belongs to no one (and certainly not the estate).' And so the sins and injustices of yesteryear are perpetuated in the present day!

After his time at Fresgill, Rob Donn enlisted in the First Regiment of the Sutherland Highlanders in 1759 and he was with them until 1763, two years after the passing of Donald, 4th Lord Reay. The Sutherlands too were undergoing dynastic change. The Earl of Sutherland died in 1766, leaving a disputed succession. This was finally resolved in 1771 in favour of the five-year-old daughter Elizabeth, who was then named Countess of Sutherland. Her succession inspired a late and famous elegy by Rob Donn. It is included as Poem Five in the Appendix. A paragraph in Ian Grimble's work on Rob Donn (published in 1979) describes the import of this work so perfectly that I am going to include it here:

> It is one of the most notorious facts of Highland history that Rob Donn's prophecy was to receive a grizzly fulfilment. After the Countess Elizabeth had married the Marquess of Stafford, that spark did blaze into a fire, spread throughout the Mackay country by the ground-officers of Patrick Sellar.
>
> The extent of the Countess Elizabeth's responsibility for what occurred remains a subject of controversy, aggravated by the suppression for over 150 years of the evidence in the Dunrobin Muniments.

This was the tragedy of the Highland Clearances, gathering like black storm clouds over Mackay country in the later years of the eighteenth century. In fact, there were many Mackays onboard the *Hector*, as she slipped out of Loch Broom, as early as 1773, heading for the Pictou River in Nova Scotia.

Long before the events of the next century broke, however, Rob Donn stepped out of this life, aged 63 years, and was buried in Balnakil churchyard in 1778. A monument in remembrance of him stands there now, in that lovely resting place in the north-west corner of the country. And beyond the ivy-covered church ruins, the sands stretch away to the north, a golden line of dunes, ending in that northern ocean that so inspired his works.

He has not been forgotten, and the people of Sutherland have preserved the old songs and the old music in written form. The first book to try to reproduce his quicksilver words was published in 1829, entitled *Orain le Rob Donn* (The Songs of Rob Donn).

I will remember him particularly by his verse in praise of Glen

Golly. It is the last word in the Appendix and is a joyous song of homage to the land.

Mary, Rob Donn's daughter, married a Donald Mackay who served in the Duke of Gordon's Fencibles. They had a daughter, Jean who, as we heard, married my great-great-great-grandfather, Donald Mackay of Achunlochie. Like his father, Donald was a cooper by trade. He and Jean moved to Reay to build a new future after he was evicted by non-renewal of his lease.

CHAPTER TEN

Change: A Double-Edged Dirk

CHANGE WAS IN THE AIR IN THE EIGHTEENTH AND nineteenth centuries. The defeat of the Jacobites at Culloden didn't cause the Highland Clearances. Emigration and social change were on the way anyway, with a certain inevitability. What the Jacobite disaster on the field that day meant, however, was that the change in question was much more brutal and happened far more quickly than would otherwise have been the case.

The land forfeitures, disarming acts and proscriptions on Highland dress led to a people unhappy at the destruction of the old ways. Ironically, however, these were the same people who were suddenly freed from the 'clan chief–tacksman' relationship and were able to make independent value judgements.

Furthermore, clan chiefs were being replaced, by act and by evolution, by landlords and estate owners. These changes led to high rents and evictions and so the emptying of the northern lands began. The disgruntled and the dispossessed found themselves travelling in company and altogether, between 1749 and 1775, tens of thousands of Highlanders left the glens to search for a better life in the New World. This first great wave of emigration comprised mainly those tacksmen who had the coin to pay for the endeavour and the strength of character to make an active choice to leave.

A George Mackay of Mudale led a party of emigrants to Carolina in 1772. The party was composed mostly of Mackay tacksmen's families and they all had enough money to buy their own land. The British Government of that time gave 50 acres of land to every emigrant that gave the oath of allegiance to Britain. None of these Mackays took the oath, and when the War of Independence broke out they were free to fight for America.

The American War of Independence lasted from 1775 until 1783. As we have heard, it was during this period that Rob Donn died. The war also caused a temporary halt to the shiploads of Highland emigrants bound for America's shores. The only Highlanders who made the crossing during those years were soldiers in the service of King George III. They were recruited in their thousands, with the main inducements to serve being permission to wear the kilt, bear arms and play the pipes. These were powerful incentives for a people whose entire culture had been dismantled and ploughed under and explains how the chiefs managed, in the latter half of the eighteenth century, to raise 22 Highland regiments for service to the crown.

In 1792 the situation intensified – the 'Big Sheep' had arrived. Sir John Sinclair of Ulbster introduced the creatures to his estate at Langwell and it seems that, as motive, he genuinely had the welfare of his tenants in view. He felt that these Cheviot sheep, with improved wool and meat yield, would improve the northern quality of life. Instead, on many estates, it became the final pressure which the people were unable to resist. And so the Clearances began in earnest, the people being replaced by sheep, which created more wealth for the landowners.

This second wave of Highland emigration was much more wretched than the first, because it was enforced and consisted of a population betrayed by those whom they had looked to for protection. Many people from Eriboll, in Mackay country, left in the 1790s, bound for Prince Edward Island, Cape Breton and

Pictou, Nova Scotia. Around this time Thomas Douglas, the 5th Earl of Selkirk, was one of the few who tried to alleviate the worst injustices of this wholesale emigration. Among other great works, he founded a planned settlement of Scots on the Red River (which later grew into the city of Winnipeg and its surrounds). Not all who were evicted left the country, however. At the close of Chapter Nine, for example, I explained how Donald and Jean Mackay were cleared from Achunlochie, but found a place to live in Reay.

The Sutherland Clearances were the most savage in the country. The first forcible evictions took place in 1807, but things really got rolling in 1809, with the arrival of William Young and Patrick Sellar. William Young was an agricultural improver and Patrick Sellar was the Procurator-Fiscal of Moray. They boarded a ship at Burghead, where they left both their honour and their human charity on the quay, and then they sailed to Sutherland. They became the commissioner and factor, respectively, on the Sutherland estates.

This was bad news for the Mackays, because over the last few years most of the ancestral lands had been sold, piece by piece, to the Sutherlands. Mackay country now began to suffer an increasing tally of evictions and a large number of Mackays left in 1813 for the Earl of Selkirk's Red River settlement. Later that same year, Young and Sellar acquired a new boss. Edinburgh lawyer James Loch was appointed senior commissioner to the Sutherland estates and he was the flint that set the north of Sutherland afire.

The year 1814 was known as 'The Year of the Burnings'. Many families and communities in Strathnaver were burned out and at least one house set aflame with knowledge of a bedridden old lady still inside. For this crime Patrick Sellar was imprisoned and tried for murder, but in 1816 a jury of his peers found him not-guilty. After he was released, the backlash was terrible. In one day only, in 1819, he made Strathnaver, land of the Aberach Mackays, into a desert. The end began at Grummore, on Loch

Naver, on a May morning, and at eleven o'clock that night an eyewitness, Donald MacLeod, could see the townships burning in a long line for more than ten miles. Three hundred buildings were burning from Grummore on the loch, north to Skail.

Another witness, young Roderick MacLeod, said, 'The terrible remembrance of the burnings of Strathnaver will live as long as a root of the people remains in the country.'

Elsewhere in the north, after the initial eviction from Achunlochie, Donald and Jean Mackay seem not to have been further bedevilled by Clearance. They had two children that we know of, Mary and David.

David, a cooper, settled in West Strathen, in Melness. One of his sons, Robert, went to Saskatchewan in Canada. There are now many descendants, both there and in Manitoba.

It is with Mary (daughter of Donald and Jean) that we will concern ourselves, though. She married John Sutherland (a crofter and agricultural worker) and they settled in Strathmelness, where all their family were born.

So who was John Sutherland? His father was Robert Sutherland, a farmer and weaver, and his mother was Janet Mackay. This Janet had been cleared, together with her father and five siblings, from Musal, in Strathmore. Many of the people of the West Moine settled in Melness during these times of Clearance. It is said in a Durness genealogical publication that the people that got crofts on Melness were nearly all from Strathmore, Hope, Heilam and Fresgill districts. They all had to start from scratch. A lot of them were soldiers who had returned from the wars to find their original homes torn down and gone. Their 6 d a day, after 24 years' service to the Crown, just about covered the rents for the poor crofts they had now to live on at the coastal Clearance settlements. The tenants of Melness who lived there before the evictions had to live on smaller crofts and try to get part of their living from the sea.

In about 1835 the Government had employed an east-coast fisherman to teach the people the white fishing industry. As the men got used to the sea they started going to the herring fishing at Wick and later to Shetland, Stornoway and Barra. The women also went to Wick to gut and pack the herring. At season's end they all returned home and undertook improvements on the crofts.

Mary Mackay and John Sutherland were married in 1837, the same year Queen Victoria was crowned. They had at least seven of a family, all born in Melness, of whom the seventh (their daughter, Grace Sutherland) was my great-grandmother. It seems appropriate, however, to fill in some biographical detail about each of Grace's siblings before learning more about her and the man she married.

James was the eldest son of Mary and John. He was born in 1838 and went to sea on a whaling ship. He was known as 'Forty' (perhaps his number on the ship). He later settled in Strath Halladale and had a holding there. When my grandfather, Willie MacDonald, was a young boy, he used to go and help his Uncle James with the sheep.

Next came Donald, born in 1841, who married a woman from Farr. He went to Glasgow and later to Bunessan on Mull, where he worked as a blacksmith. Some of the family may still be there, but one of his daughters came back to Farr, married and settled. Members of that family still live in Farr and in Tongue.

Janet was third and was born in 1842. She married William Campbell, a tailor in Thurso, and they had seven or eight of a family.

The fourth child, Robert, became a very well-known piper during the nineteenth century. He was a pipe major in the Highland Light Infantry. He composed many tunes including 'Talmine Bay', 'The Melness Braes' and many others. My mother is still tracking down some of his compositions today.

Next came George, who married Barbara MacLeod and settled in Melness.

The sixth child is more of a mystery. My mother thinks that it was a daughter, as Grace allegedly had a sister who went to

Glasgow and then married and settled there. My mother is also ever hopeful about finding more about this grand-aunt of hers.

Grace was born in 1851. As we have heard, conditions had been very harsh in the crofting areas in the century since Culloden. She went, along with the other young women of her time, to the herring ports for work, gutting and packing the herring. This was seasonal work, rather than permanent employment, so she also worked as an agricultural worker. This was a common occupation amongst the young unmarried women. After this she went into domestic service, working as a housekeeper in Glasgow.

It was in 1875 while Grace was in Glasgow, aged about 24, that her father John Sutherland died in Strathen, Melness. He was aged 70 and had suffered from heart disease and pneumonia. She was still in service in Glasgow, eight years later, when she married merchant seaman Hugh MacDonald in 1883.

It isn't known where Grace and Hugh first met, but it can be fun to speculate! Perhaps in Melness, where many of his relations lived. Perhaps in Fraserburgh, when she would have been working at the herring and he would be home between voyages. Or perhaps in Glasgow, while she was in service and where he sometimes had shore leave.

This Hugh MacDonald is the one foretold in Chapter Eight – the descendant of Alasdair Carrach, Keppoch chief of the Clanranalds of Lochaber. George MacDonald of the Lochaber Clanranalds had come north to Durness late in the seventeenth century, as a follower of Munro of Coul. In 1772, all of his descendants, except one grandson (also called George) emigrated to Carolina. This grandson, George, took his wife and family to live at Strathmelness, at a place called Achintihalavan (meaning 'place of the underground houses'). This, of course, was beside a prehistoric site.

Hugh MacDonald, Grace Sutherland's new husband, was George's great-grandson and although he had been born in Fraserburgh in 1846, he still had many relatives back in Melness.

After their wedding she moved to Aberdeen and Hugh went back to sea. Their first child, Mary, was born in Aberdeen in 1884. Grace went to Melness when her daughter Mary was just a toddler, and the rest of their family – Hughie, Willie and Johnnie – were all born there. In 1896, a year after the birth of his youngest son, Johnnie, and at the age of 50, Hugh decided to settle ashore. His first position was as a labourer at the building of Talmine Pier. However, he suffered a serious accident during this job. A crane collapsed and he sustained a back injury which was to cause him difficulties for the rest of his life and compelled him to stay close to home.

The family all stayed in Strathen with Grace's mother, Mary, who lived to see 86 years. She may then have had a stroke, because her death certificate says that she had paralysis for ten days. She died in 1901, which was the same year that Queen Victoria died, and Edward VII and II came to the throne.

Of her three MacDonald grandsons, only the eldest, Hughie, who had been born in 1888, was old enough to have suffered the human injustice of ethnic suppression. I remember speaking with Hughie, who was known to my generation as 'the Old Timer'. I was probably too young to see the full import of his story at the time, but 'The Tale of the Black Block' has always stayed with me.

The people had, for 150 years, been forbidden by the Government to speak their native language. This was even the case in schools, where children were punished harshly for speaking Gaelic – each morning the headmaster gave one child some object, which was known as 'a token'. When the first child heard another speaking a word of Gaelic the token (sometimes a black block) was passed on to that child, who later passed it on to any other who would dare to speak in his native tongue. At the end of the day the headmaster took in the token and every child who had received it during the day was severely punished with the belt.

This practice had ceased by the time Willie went to school

and it is a triumph, really, that Gaelic, tartan, kilts and pipes all survive today in spite of such past cultural persecutions. All three of the MacDonald boys were keen to see action in the First World War. However, Hughie, the eldest, was sent home from Portsmouth by the navy, rejected on the grounds of poor eyesight. Johnnie enlisted in the Scots Guards, where Willie was already serving. Johnnie rapidly gained promotion, soon becoming the youngest pipe major in the Scots Guards.

It was during the war in 1915, that their father, Hugh MacDonald died, aged 69, of stomach cancer. It was during the same war, in 1917, that Mary, now 32, married John MacKinnon from Skye. By the following year she was pregnant and by November 1918 both she and the child were dead.

Fate had thrown them into the path of that huge, but formless, killer – the post-war flu epidemic that took so many. Her death certificate reads:

> Heart failure following epidemic influenza and exhaustion after delivery of a premature child, born 7–11–1918.

To make the tragedy even worse, John MacKinnon, devastated at the loss of his wife and child, disappeared completely. Despite efforts by Mary's family, he was never found.

Back in Melness, Grace survived her daughter by a further 12 years. Her sons built her a new house in Midtown after the war. She lived there with her son Hughie and later Willie brought his wife there to live too. Grace became very rheumatic during the last few years of her life. She died in 1931 in that house in Melness where my mother had been born nearly seven years previously.

Grace and Hugh's eldest son, Hughie, was a labourer by trade and he was employed, all his life, as a roadman with Sutherland County Council.

Like his two younger brothers he was very musical, playing

both the pipes and violin. In middle age, he married Elizabeth Clark of Rosehall. Sadly he lost her to throat cancer within six years and they had no children. Hughie lived on in Gruids, until his death from a stroke in 1966.

Grace and Hugh's youngest son, Johnnie, became one of the best-known pipers in the first half of the twentieth century. Known as J.D. MacDonald in the piping world, so as to distinguish him from the other leading pipers by the same name, he won all the leading piping awards.

J.D.'s time in the piping limelight coincided with George V's time on the throne, which was a happy circumstance. George V was very fond of the bagpipes, and this mutual enthusiasm was the basis for a friendship of sorts between these two. J.D. became known as 'The King's Piper'.

This obviously put him in a privileged position for such a pipe major and he was able to introduce some new developments. The first of these was in the late 1920s and was the inclusion of a pipe band in the Changing-of-the-Guard ceremony in London. The second development was the invention of the now commonplace procedure of the pipe band marching and counter-marching. In 1930, the King received J.D. in private at Buckingham Palace and presented him with the Royal Victorian Medal. This is a special award, which can be given only by the monarch. The King also took the opportunity to express his pleasure at being able to reward him on this occasion for his piping services to the Crown. He met and married in London. His wife was a nurse from Islay, by the name of Marion McTaggart and known by the Gaelic Morag. He was discharged from the army after contracting tuberculosis and spent six months in a sanatorium in the Isle of Wight. After this, though, he returned, first to Melness, and later to Lairg, with his wife and family. He died in 1946, aged 50, and the Scots Guards sent floral tributes.

The middle son of Hugh and Grace MacDonald, was, as we have heard, William MacDonald. Grace has been described as a very cheerful lady and full of fun. She was very musical and her house was one of the well-known houses for evenings of storytelling and music.

All of her sons inherited her gift for music and Willie was particularly interested in all things traditional. He loved the bagpipes, pipe music, Gaelic songs, Highland dancing and other aspects of the Gaelic culture. He knew the story of every piobaireachd and was an exponent of *Canntaireachd* (the art of teaching pipe music by special oral sounds – which was the system in the days before written music). He was also a prolific composer of pipe music.

I remember him sitting with me on a bench at the gable of the house in Gruids. My cousin John said to me recently that he thought that the one thing Willie didn't plan on was leaving us so early. He died at the age of 71 in 1963. I remember him telling me stories – and I'm glad I got that chance.

The stories of the seanachaidh tell people who they are, where they came from, their place in the land or the land's place in them. The seanachaidh was cultural bedrock. The liquid that flowed around this bedrock was the music. It flowed from voices, fiddles and especially the pipes. There was a piper in Melness, a great piper, and native of the place, named William MacDonald.

He could feel the land beneath his feet and he passed a lot of that on to others, through dry humour. He and his people had been in the land, and of the land, since time before time. The histories related that Willie was descended from Conn, who reigned in Ulster from 123 until 173 and from Colla, who was Conn's great-great-grandson and Lord of Dalriada, the first major settlement in the west of Alba.

Willie was also my grandfather.

The people described in chapters Nine and Ten are illustrated by Table 6, page 157.

EPILOGUE

The Binding

THIS IS THE TODAY AND THE TOMORROW OF MY TALE, AND how it stands with all the other tales. I was born by Ben Nevis in 1960, the youngest of four siblings, and our home place was in the crofting township of Tomonie. I grew up there, and took joy in the turning of the year. The mountain stood, large and constant to the south, but its look changed with the seasons. It was like a marker for us. A measure of passing time.

Even in winter the Ben was rarely white to its feet, for the Gulf Stream warmed us. But when we did get snow, it was out with the sledges and onto the slopes. Spring, when the mountain was green and blue, was a time for long cycle runs on the single-track roads through the glens. And as I got older, spring and summer weekends also meant taking part in that cherished pastime, hill-walking, with my father and his friends. We undertook these expeditions in the autumn too, but that often tended, unfortunately, to become a more than damp pursuit. Autumn would turn the Ben brown and purple, when it could be seen at all through that curious Lochaber phenomenon, horizontal rain. Despite the weather, I did enjoy helping friends on Locheilside with the autumn gathering of the flocks from the hills.

And then the Ben would turn grey-black and it would be darkest winter again until Hogmanay. Then, at midnight, we would hear the guns of neighbours being fired and my father playing the pipes at the gable of the house, welcoming in another year.

I went to Glasgow University in the late 1970s and studied Geography and Scottish History. I was lucky in my professional life, securing employment in the fields of tourism and cultural heritage. I have worked for tourist boards and local councils. I have, myself, been an expatriot for brief periods, working in Vermont and in New York State, and helping to organise Moscow's first Highland Games.

At the time of this writing, I am employed by the National Trust for Scotland at Culloden Battlefield. It is a stirring place to be, but a hard place too. It's one of those locations where both the fire and the melancholy of the Celt are at their most intense. But it's also a lodestone, drawing the people of the diaspora back from across the globe with a relentless pull. Our doors open, time and again, to emigrant-descendants from all over the world, many of them with stories more remarkable than the one you have been reading.

One man brought us the ship's manifest from the *Hector,* which sailed to Nova Scotia in 1773, and told us tales from the emigrants' song.

Another is descended from Jacobite prisoner and Cherokee/Shawnee Indian, and now offers storytelling for us. He is blessed to feel the land of two continents breathing beneath his feet.

Still a third only came in because he had the time to check out a far-fetched story of his grandfather's – what he found was that it was accurate in its every wrinkle. These, and dozens more, contrive to stir the blood and they create an obligation. I have read some emigrant tales that bring tears every few pages.

We, none of us, live alone.

Our tales are intertwined and to have a tale that touches other lives and then not to tell it is to live in darkness.

There are other motivations too, in the telling of this tale.

This narrative stretches across centuries of difficulties with our southern neighbour, England.

There is therefore a sense of rightness and of closure to be writing this just three years after the creation of a Scottish Parliament. There are more than a few of those who came before who will be smiling to see that. And in the same vein, the holding of festivals, such as American Tartan Day on 6 April each year, all help to increase our sense of national self-respect. This has been low since the proscriptions after Culloden, but now a new breeze is blowing through.

This renaissance in the Scottish spirit should also increase our awareness of the importance of the land. After all, when it is understood that you are just a guardian, in a long line of guardians, then your respect for your charge rises accordingly.

This land is not ours to do with as we please – rather, we belong to the land, and it is a duty handed down to us to look after it. Our aim should be to pass it on to those who are to come in no worse state than we received it – and in a better condition when we can.

My tale is not unusual. Everyone has a family that stretches as far, and farther, back. The only people I have ever heard of who don't have a family line that goes as far back as mine are Pinocchio and Frankenstein's monster. I'm just lucky, because I know the details, thanks to my mother's work.

Knowing then, that it was a tale for telling, and perhaps an encouragement to others, I felt moved to take out my mother's research. I have chosen only some strands out of many, blended them with the appropriate tales I have heard throughout my life and verified it all against scholarly sources. The end product is our tale. Our gift to the book of all tales. I hope you have enjoyed it!

Family Tree Appendix

TABLE 1. THE EARLIEST WORD (123–474 – PART ONE)

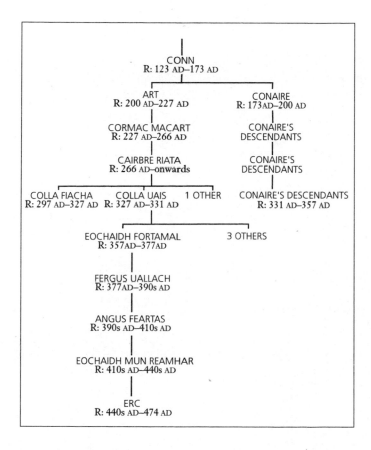

TABLE 1. THE EARLIEST WORD (474–843 – PART TWO)

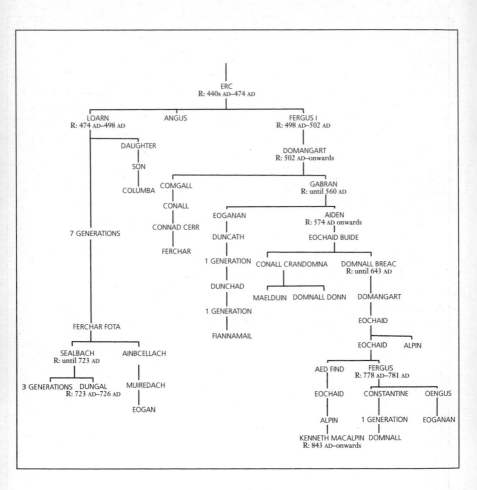

TABLE 2. NATIONHOOD AND SHAKESPEARE (843–1124)

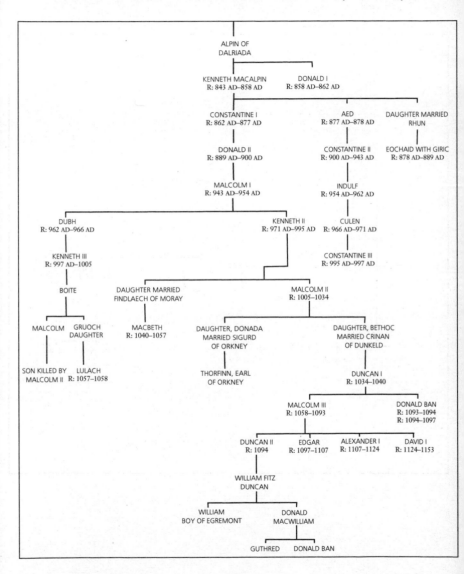

TABLE 3. SUCCESSION WARS AND STEWARTS (1124–1412)

Includes no claimants from illegitimate children, and remaining claimants are set in italic

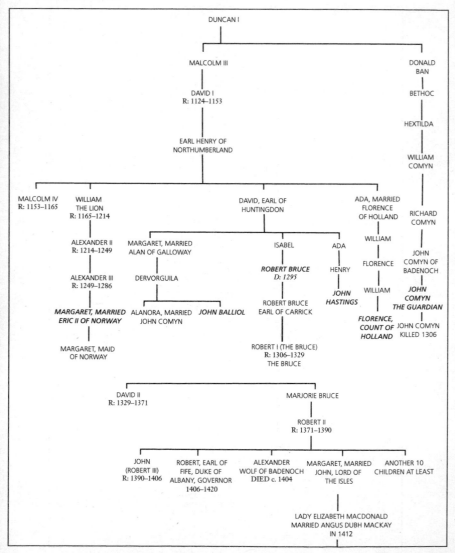

TABLE 4. SUMMARY TIME MAP (123–1412)

How to get from Conn of the Hundred Battles to Elizabeth MacDonald and Angus Dubh Mackay

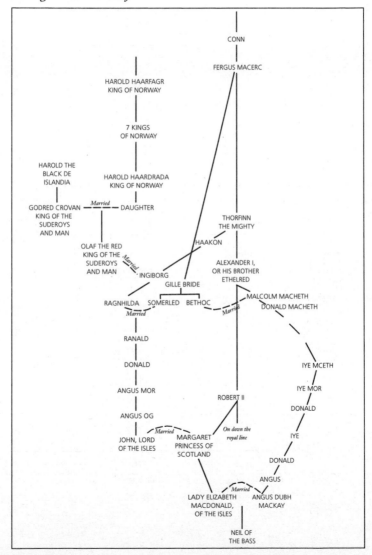

TABLE 5. MOSTLY MACKAYS (1365–1700)

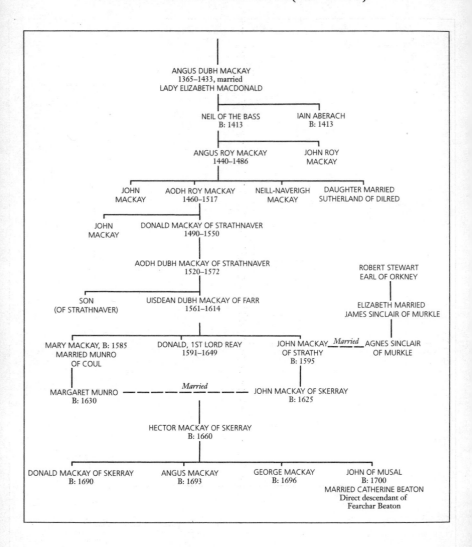

ANGUS DUBH MACKAY
1365–1433, married
LADY ELIZABETH MACDONALD

NEIL OF THE BASS
B: 1413

IAIN ABERACH
B: 1413

ANGUS ROY MACKAY
1440–1486

JOHN ROY
MACKAY

JOHN
MACKAY

AODH ROY MACKAY
1460–1517

NEILL-NAVERIGH
MACKAY

DAUGHTER MARRIED
SUTHERLAND OF DILRED

JOHN
MACKAY

DONALD MACKAY OF STRATHNAVER
1490–1550

AODH DUBH MACKAY OF STRATHNAVER
1520–1572

ROBERT STEWART
EARL OF ORKNEY

SON
(OF STRATHNAVER)

UISDEAN DUBH MACKAY OF FARR
1561–1614

ELIZABETH MARRIED
JAMES SINCLAIR OF MURKLE

MARY MACKAY, B: 1585
MARRIED MUNRO
OF COUL

DONALD, 1ST LORD REAY
1591–1649

JOHN MACKAY *Married* AGNES SINCLAIR
OF STRATHY   OF MURKLE
B: 1595

MARGARET MUNRO ——————— *Married* ——————— JOHN MACKAY OF SKERRAY
B: 1630   B: 1625

HECTOR MACKAY OF SKERRAY
B: 1660

DONALD MACKAY OF SKERRAY
B: 1690

ANGUS MACKAY
B: 1693

GEORGE MACKAY
B: 1696

JOHN OF MUSAL
B: 1700
MARRIED CATHERINE BEATON
Direct descendant of
Fearchar Beaton

TABLE 6. UP TO THE PRESENT (1660–2004)

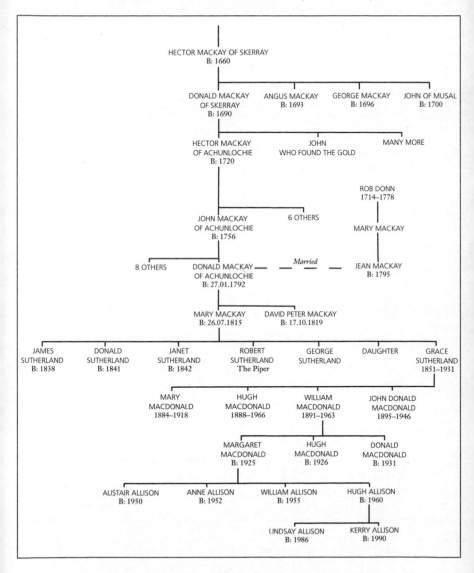

HECTOR MACKAY OF SKERRAY
B: 1660

DONALD MACKAY OF SKERRAY B: 1690   ANGUS MACKAY B: 1693   GEORGE MACKAY B: 1696   JOHN OF MUSAL B: 1700

HECTOR MACKAY OF ACHUNLOCHIE B: 1720   JOHN WHO FOUND THE GOLD   MANY MORE

ROB DONN 1714–1778

JOHN MACKAY OF ACHUNLOCHIE B: 1756   6 OTHERS

MARY MACKAY

8 OTHERS   DONALD MACKAY OF ACHUNLOCHIE B: 27.01.1792   *Married*   JEAN MACKAY B: 1795

MARY MACKAY B: 26.07.1815   DAVID PETER MACKAY B: 17.10.1819

JAMES SUTHERLAND B: 1838   DONALD SUTHERLAND B: 1841   JANET SUTHERLAND B: 1842   ROBERT SUTHERLAND The Piper   GEORGE SUTHERLAND   DAUGHTER   GRACE SUTHERLAND 1851–1931

MARY MACDONALD 1884–1918   HUGH MACDONALD 1888–1966   WILLIAM MACDONALD 1891–1963   JOHN DONALD MACDONALD 1895–1946

MARGARET MACDONALD B: 1925   HUGH MACDONALD B: 1926   DONALD MACDONALD B: 1931

ALISTAIR ALLISON B: 1950   ANNE ALLISON B: 1952   WILLIAM ALLISON B: 1955   HUGH ALLISON B: 1960

LINDSAY ALLISON B: 1986   KERRY ALLISON B: 1990

The Bard's Appendix

ONE

Gu Bheil Mis' air mo Phianadh
'N uair theid am fadar thoirt dachaidh
Is a steach thun na spreidhe,
Gu 'm bi ise 'g a shireadh
Aig a' mhionaid 's d' an leir dhi;
Ma bhios bad ann gun bhualadh
Ann am buaireadh gu 'n leum i,
'S gu 'm bi sud ann mo choinneamh-s'
Mur dean na bollachan eirigh.

Ma theid graine dheth 'n diuchaidh,
No ma bheir luchag de 'n chailbhe,
Canaidh ise le as-caoin
Gu bheil rud as d' a cuid arbhair;
Bidh mi fhein is mo chaiptean
Ann an tarsunnachd shearbha,
'S ged nach fhaighinn ach forlach,
Bhithinn deonach air falbh uaith'.

159

'N uair a chunntas i suas dhomh
Na h-uile suaineach is teadhair,
'S mise dh'fheumas bhi cuimhneach
Mu na buill sin a ghleidheil.
'N uair a shin i le ruathar,
Is mi shuas ann an cathair,
Ghabh mi aithreachas gabhaidh,
'S ann a dh'fhag mi a gleadhar.

Ach na 'n tigeadh am faghair,
Cha bhiodh draghais na suist orm,
Cha bhiodh curam a ceannach,
Ged nach biodh bannach 's an duthaich.
Cha bhiodh eader a Ghlais-bheinn
Agus Eas-coire Dughaill
Ceum nach fhaodainn-s' a shireadh.

What torment I will suffer
When the fodder is taken home
And carried in for the cattle,
Herself will be examining it
At the first opportunity.
If there should be a sheaf unthreshed
What a rage she will fly into,
And I will be for it
If the bolls do not increase in number.

If a grain of it is destroyed,
Even what a small mouse would take
into a wattle-wall,
she says angrily
That some of her corn is missing.
I and my captain will be
Bickering bitterly,
And though I only got a furlough
I would gladly leave her.

When she makes an inventory
Of all the plough reins and tethers
It's up to me to remember
To look after all those ropes.
When she launched an attack on me
As I was sitting in a chair
I was filled with alarm
And I fled from her din.

But if autumn would come
I would not be wielding the flail.
There would be no concern about commerce,
Even if there weren't a bannock in the land.
There would not be a step between the grey hill:
And the waterfall in Dougall's Corrie
That I wouldn't be at liberty to follow.

TWO

Is Trom Leam an Airigh
Is trom leam an airigh 's a' ghair seo a th'innt',
Gun a' phairtinn a dh'fhag mi bhith 'n drasd air
mo chinn:
Anna chaol-mhalach chioch-chorrach shliob-
cheannach chruinn,
Is Iseabail a' bheoil mhilis, mhanranach bhinn.
Heich! Mar a bha, air mo chin,
A dh'fhag mi cho craiteach 's nach stath dhomh
bhith 'g inns'.

Shiubhail mis' a' bhuaile 's suas feadh nan
craobh,
'S gach ait' anns am b'abhaist bhith pagadh mo
ghaoil;
Nuair chunnaic mi 'm fear ban ud 's e manran r'a
mhnaoi,
B'fhearr leam nach tiginn idir laimh riu, no 'n
gaoith
'Se mar a bha, air mo chinn,
A dh'fhag mi cho craiteach 's nach stath dhomh
bhith 'g inns'.

On chualas gun gluaiseadh tu uam leis an t-Saor
Tha mo shuain air a buaireadh le bruadraichean
gaoil;
De 'n chairdeas a bha siud chan fhair mi bhith
saor,
Gun bharnaigeadh laimh riut tha 'n gradh dhomh
'na mhaor,
Air gach trath, 's mi ann an stri,
A' feuchainn r'a aicheadh 's e fas rium mar
chraoibh.

Ach Anna bhuidh' Ni'n Domhnaill, nam b'eol
　　duit mo ni,
'Se do ghradh gun bhith paight' leag a-bhan uam
　　mo chli;
Tha e dhomh a t'fhianais cho gniomhach 's nuair
　　chi,
Diogalladh, 's a' smusach, gur ciurrtach mo chridh.
Nis, ma tha mi ga do dhith
Gum b'fheairrde mi pag uait mus fagainn an tir.

Ach labhair I gu faiteagach, ailgheasach rium:
'Chan fhair thu bhith laimh rium do charadh mo
　　chinn;
Tha sianar gam iarraidh o bhliadhna do thim,
'S cha b'araidh le cach thu, thoirt barr os an
　　cinn.
Ha, ha, ha! An d'fhas thu gu tinn,
'N e 'n gaol a bheir bas ort? Gum paigh thu d'a
　　chin!'

Ach cionnas bheir mi fuath dhuit, ged
　　dh'fhuaraich thu rium?
Nuair's feargaich mo sheanchas mu t'ainm air
　　do chul,
Thig t'iomhaigh le h-annsachd 'na shamhladh
　　'nam uidh,
Saoilidh mi an sin gun dean an gaol sin an turn,
'S theid air a rath gu h-as-ur,
Is fasaidh e 'n trath sin cho-arda ri tur.

The Sheiling is a sad place for me

The shieling is a sad place for me, when the
　　present company in it —
Rather than the company who used to be there -
　　are near to me —

Anna of the passionate breast, finely arched
    brows, shining hair, style;
And honey-mouthed Isabel, melodious, sweet.
Alas for things as they were at the back of my croft –
I have grown so bereft, there is no point in
    talking about it.

I wandered across the fold and up into the woods
And everywhere I used to caress my love.
When I saw that fair fellow courting his wife
I wish I had not come near them or beside them.
That's how it was behind my croft
To make me so dispirited – though it's shameful
    to sing about it.

'Fair Anna, Donald's daughter, if you knew my
    condition,
It is unrequited love for you that deprived me of
    my reason.
It remains as lively with me as in your presence,
Teasing and provoking, wounding me to the
    heart.
All through the day I am in turmoil,
Trying to quench it, while it grows in me like a
    tree.'

But she spoke very disdainfully, superciliously to
    me,
'You don't deserve to be beside me, stroking my
    head.
Six men have been seeking me since the year of
    your courtship
And the others would hardly expect you to
    surpass them.
Ha! Ha! Ha! Are you deranged?

If it's love that will cause your death, you are
   going to pay for it.'

'But how can I hate you, even though you have
   grown so cold to me?
Whenever I disparage your name behind your
   back
Your image floats with its fascination as an
   embodiment of my dreams
So that I will conceive love to be that which will
   never alter,
And this is proved as it wells up again
And it grows then as high as a tower.

Since it was rumoured that you would forsake me
   for the carpenter
My sleep is disturbed with dreams of love.
Of the affection that was between us I cannot
   break free:
When I am not beside you, love is like a bailiff to
   me.
But if I am to be without you
It would do me good to get a kiss from you before
   you leave the district.'

THREE

Oran nan Casaga Dubha
Faire, faire, Righ Deorsa!
'N ann a' spors' air do dhilsean,
'Deanamh achdachan ura
Gu bhi dublachadh 'n daorsa;
Ach, o 's balaich gun uails' iad,
'S fearr am bualadh no 'n caomhnadh,
'S bidh na 's lugha 'g ad fheitheamh
'N uair thig a leithid a ris oirnn.

Ma gheobh do namhaid 's do charaid
An aon pheanas an Albainn,
'S iad a dh'eirich 'n ad aghaidh
'Rinn an roghainn a b'fhearra dhiubh;
Oir tha caraid math cuil ac'
A rinn taobh ris na dh' earb ris,
'S a' chuid nach d'imich do'n Fhrainc leis,
Fhuair iad pension 'n uair dh'fhalbh e.

Och, mo thruaighe sin Albainn!
'S tur a dhearbh sibh bhur reason;
Gur i 'n rain bh'ann bhur n-inntinn
'N rud a mhill air gach gleus sibh;
Leugh an gobharmad sannt
Anns gach neach a theanndaidh ris fein dhibh,
'S thug iad baoight do bhur gionaich,
Gu 'r cur fo mhionach a cheile.

Ghlac na Sasunnaich fath oirbh
Gus bhur fagail na 's laige,
Chum 's nach bithteadh 'g ur cunntadh
'N ur luchd-comh-stri na b'fhaide;

Ach 'n uair a bhios sibh a dh'easbhuidhe
Bhur n-airm, 's bhur n-acfhuinnean sraide,
Gheobh sibh searsaigeadh mionaich,
Is bidh bhur peanas na 's graide.

Tha mi 'faicinn bhur truaighe,
Mar ni nach cualas a shamhuil;
A' chuid a 's fearr de bhur seabh'gan,
Bhi air slabhruidh aig clamhan;
Ach ma tha sibh 'n ar leomhann,
Pillibh 'n doghruinn-s' 'n a teamhair,
'S deanaibh 'n deudach a thrusadh,
Mu's teid ur busan a cheangal.

Nis, a Thearlaich oig Stiubhaird,
Ruit tha duil aig gach fine,
Chaidh a chothachadh cruin dhuit,
'S a leig an duthaich 'n a teine;
Tha mar nathraichean falaicht',
A chaill an earradh an uiridh,
Ach tha 'g ath-ghleusadh an gathan
Gu eirigh latha do thighinn.

'S iomadh neach a tha guidheadh
Ri do thighinn, a Thearlaich,
Gus an eireadh na cuinghean
Dhe na bhuidheann tha 'n eiginn;
A tha 'cantuinn 'n an cridhe,
Ged robh an teanga 'g a bhreugadh,
'Lan do bheatha gu t' fhaicinn,
A dh'ionnsuidh Bhreatainn is Eirinn.'

'S iomadh oganach aimsicht'
Tha 's an am so 'n a chadal,
Eader braighe Srath-Chluanaidh

Agus bruachan Loch-Abair
Rachadh 'n cuisibh mhic t' athar,
'S a chrun, 's a chaithir r' an tagradh,
'S a dh' ath-philleadh na ceathairn
A dhioladh latha Chul-odair.

Ma 's e 'm peacach a 's mugha
'S coir a chumhachd a chlaoidheadh:
Nach e Seumas an seachdamh
Dhearbh bhi seasmhach 'n a inntinn?
C' uim' an diteadh sibh 'n onoir,
Na bhiodh sibh moladh na daoidheachd?
'S gur h-e dhluitheachd d' a chreidimh
A thug do choigrich an rioghachd.

Fhuair sinn Righ a Hanobhar:
Sparradh oirnne le h-achd e;
Tha againn Prionnsa 'n a aghaidh,
Is neart an lagha 'g a bhacadh:
O Bhith tha h-urad 'n ad bhritheamh,
Gun chron 's an dithis nach fac thu,-
Mur h-e a th' ann, cuir air adhairt
An t-aon a 's lugha 'm bi 'pheacadh.

Song of a long black coat
So, so King George!
What a mockery of your good faith
To make new laws
That double the bondage.
But since they are fellows without honour
It would be better to strike than spare,
And there will be fewer to support you
When the same thing happens again.

If your enemy and your friend
Receive the same punishment in Scotland,
Those who rose against you
Made the better choice;
For they have a good friend behind them
Who stood by those who trusted him,
And several who did not go to France with him
Received pensions when he left.

O my pity for you, Scotland!
How your argument is proved
That the part you chose
Has been your ruin in every respect.
Observe the Government's meanness
Towards all who supported it
While they have given you a bait
That will tear your entrails apart.

The English have taken the opportunity
To leave you weakened
So that you will not be accounted
As warriors any longer.
But when you are lacking
Your weapons and your equipment
You will receive a thorough frisking
And your punishment will be all the swifter.

I see your misery
As something unprecedented –
The best part of your hawks
Chained to a kite.
But if you are lions
Retaliate in good time,
And have your teeth ready
Before your mouths are muzzled.

Now, young Charles Stewart,
Every clan places its hope in you
That sought to crown you
And set the country alight.
They are like serpents in hiding
Which cast their skins last year
But are making ready their fangs
To arise on the day of your coming.

Many a man is beseeching
You to come, Charles,
To lift the yokes
From those who are oppressed,
Who say in their hearts
Though their tongues may lie,
'Godspeed till we see you
Back in Britain and Ireland.'

Many a young hero
Who is now sleeping
Between the braes of Strath Cluanie
And the banks of Lochaber
Would support the cause of your father's son
In your claim to the crown and the throne,
And the troops would return
To avenge the day of Culloden.

If it be the greater sinner
Whose power ought to be overthrown,
Was it not James the Seventh
Who proved steadfast in mind?
Whose honour would you impugn
If you would praise the worthless?
It was his faith in his creed
That gave strangers the kingdom.

We acquired a King from Hanover,
Established over us by statute.
We have a Prince opposing him
In defiance of the law.
O God who is the judge,
Who sees neither as faultless,
May he put forward
The one whose sins are the less.

FOUR

Briogais Mhic Ruairidh
An d'fhidir no 'n d'fhairich no 'n cuala sibh
Co idir thug briogais Mhic Ruairidh leis?
Bha 'bhriogais ud againn an am dol a chadal
'S nuair thainig a' mhadainn cha d'fhuaireadh i.

Chaidh 'bhriogais a stampadh am meadhon na
    connlaich,
'S chaidh Huistein a dhanns leis na gruagaichibh,
'S nuair dh'fhag a chuid misg e gun tug e 'n sin
    briosgadh
A dh'iarraidh na briogais, 's cha d'fhuair e i.

Nam bitheadh tu laimh ris gun deanadh tu gaire,
Ged a bhiodh siataig sa' chruachan agad.
Na faiceadh tu dhronnag nuair dh'ionndrain e 'pheallag,
'S e coimhead 's gach callaid 's a' suaithteachan.

Iain Mhic Eachainn, mas tusa thug leat i,
Chur grabadh air peacadh 's air buaireadh leath',
Mas tu a thug leat i cha ruigeadh tu leas e,
Chaidh t'uair-sa seachad mun d'fhuair thu i.

Chaitriona Ni'n Uilleim, dean briogais do'n ghille,
'S na cumadh siud sgilinn a thuarasdal;
Ciod am fios nach e t'athair thug leis i g'a
    caitheamh-
Bha feum air a leithid 's bha uair dhe sin.

Briogais a' chonais chaidh chall air a' bhanais,
Bu liutha fear fanaid na fuaigheil oirr';
Mur do ghleidh Iain Mac Dhomhnaill gu pocan
    do'n or i
Cha robh an Us-mhoine na luaidheadh i.

Mur do ghleidh Iain Mac Dhomhnaill gu pocan
    do'n or i
Cha robh an Us-mhoine na ghluaiseadh i.
Mu Uilleam Mac Phadraig, cha deanadh I stath dha,
Cha ruigeadh i 'n aird air a' chruachan dha.

Tha duine 'n Us-mhoine d'an ainm Iain Mac
    Sheorais,
'S gur iongantas dhomhsa ma ghluais e i;
Bha i cho cumhang, mur cuir e i 'm mudhadh,
Nach dean i nas mutha na buarach dha.

Na leigibh ri braigh e 'm feadh 's a bhios e mar tha e
Air eagal gun saraich an luachair e;
Na leigibh o bhail' e do mhointeach nan coileach
Mun tig an labhallan 's gum buail i e.

(Chan eil fitheach no feannag no iolair no clamhan,
No nathair a' ghlinne 'na cuachanan
No smagach an luisean, ged 's graineil an cuspair,
Nach b'fhearr leo na musaidh do shuaitheadh riu.)

Nam faiceadh sibh 'leithid, bha bann oirr' do leathar,
Bha toll air a speathar 's bha tuathag air,
'S bha feum aic' air cobhair mu bhreidean a gobhail
Far am biodh (am ball odhar) a' suathadh rith'.

Ach Iain Mhic Choinnich 'sann ort a bha 'n sonas,
Ged 's mor a bha dhonadas sluaigh an seo,
Nuair bha thu cho sgiobalt 's nach do chaill thu dad
    idir
'S gur tapaidh a' bhriogais a bhuannaich thu!

The trousers of Rory's son
chorus:
Did you divine or detect or hear
Who on earth carried off the trousers of Rory's son?
Those trousers when we went to sleep,
and when morning came they were gone.

verses:
The breeks were trampled
amongst the straw
and Hugh went dancing with
the lassies.
When his intoxication left him
He took a bound
In search of his trousers
And couldn't find them.

If you had been near him,
You would have laughed
Even if you had rheumatism
In your hip-joints,
To have seen his loins
When he missed his covering,
And he searching in every corner
And shrugging his shoulders.

Iain Mac Eachainn,
If you carried them off
To prevent sin
And remove temptation,
If you took them
You had no need to.
You had had your day
Before you found them.

Catherine, William's Daughter,
Make some trousers for the lad
And don't take a penny
In payment for them.
Who knows but it was your father
Who took them to wear?
He needed as much
And time was when he would have done it.

The trousers whose loss
Caused friction at the wedding –
There were more mockers
Than there were patches on them.
Unless John son of Donald kept them
To make pouches for the gold,
There weren't in West Moine
Enough people to waulk them.

Unless John son of Donald made
Pouches for the gold of them,
There weren't in West Moine
Enough people to waulk them.
As for William son of Patrick,
They would be no use to him –
They wouldn't reach
Up to his hips.

There's a man in West Moine
Called John son of George
And I wouldn't be surprised
If he walked off with them.
They were so tight
That unless he alters them
They will be more like
Cow-fetters on him.

Don't let him out on the braes
In his present condition,
For fear he will be vexed
By the bulrushes.
Don't let him leave home
For the moors or the woods
Lest the water-shrew come
And nip him.

There's not a raven or crow
Or eagle or buzzard
Or serpent of the glen
In its coils,
Nor creeping things in the plants –
Though the subject's disgusting –
That they wouldn't prefer to the nasty fellow
Rubbing against them.

If you saw any like them,
They had a leather belt.
There was a hole on the fly
And a patch on it,
And it needed repairs
To the cloth of the breech
Where the dun member
Used to rub against it.

John, son of Kenneth,
You're the one who was lucky –
Though there were a lot of bad
People here –
When you were so adroit
That you never lost a thing
And so smart over the trousers
You won.

FIVE

Marbhrann do 'n Iarla Chatach
Rugadh mis' anns a' gheamhradh,
Measg nam beanntaidhnean gruamach;
'S mo cheud sealladh do 'n t-saoghal,
Sneachd is gaoth mu mo chluasaibh
O 'n chaidh m' arach ri aghaidh
Tir na deighe, gu tuathail,
Rinn mi luathaireach tuiteam,
'S rinn mo chuislidhean fuaradh'.

Chrioch mi sgur de na daintibh,
Chionn mo thalann bhi geilleadh;
Ach cha 'n fhuil'ngeadh mo nadur
Dhomh, bhi 'n am thamh air an aobhar-s',-
Ceannard Teaghlaich Dhun-Robain,
'N a luidhe 'n Abaid Dhun-eidinn,
Gun aon fhocal aig filidh
Deant' 'n a shiorraidheachd fein da.

Bha dealbh eile gu h-uasal
Air chur suas aig a dheas-laimh,
Is ann leamsa nach neonach,
An sluagh bhi bronach an Cataobh;
O na chaill iad an lanan,
Bha min, mordhalach, maiseach,
Iarla Uilleam an Coirneal,
'S a cheil' og, Mairi Macsual.

Bha mi coimeas nan armunn,
Ri deadh amhainn bha feumail,
An deigh a teine a bhathadh,
'S gun bhi lathair ach eubhall;

Ach tha mi fathast an earbsadh,
Am beagan aimsir 'n deigh so,
Gu 'm bi an t-sradag ud, Beataidh,
'N a teine lasarach aoibhian.

'N uair a bha thu 'n ad leanabh,
'S tu a dh'uireasbhuidh aimsir,
Thoisich fabhor is fortan
Ri cur casg air luchd d'ainmeinn';
Bha do thaoitearan tapaidh,
'S cobhair Freasdail 'g an leanmhuinn;
Chaill do naimhdean am barail, -
Ghleidh thu t'fhearann is t'ainmean.

Bidh mi dunadh an dain so,
Oir tha e ard air son m' inntinn;
Le aon athchuing do 'n oigh so,
Dh'fhuireach beo mar aon chuimhne:
Tha mi 'g earsadh ri Freasdal,
'S a righ gu 'm faic, 's gu 'n cluinn mi,
Thu bhi posda ri gaisgeach,
A leanas cleachd'an do shinnsear.

Elegy to the Earl of Sutherland

I was born in the winter
Among the lowering mountains;
And my first sight of the world
Snow, and wind about my ears.
Since I grew up looking upon
A land of ice, a northerly land,
I declined early
And my veins chilled.

I made an end of composing poetry
Because my talent was forsaking me;

But my nature would not allow me
To remain silent on this theme –
The head of the family of Dunrobin
Lying in the abbey at Edinburgh
Without one word from a poet
Being composed for him in his own country.

There was another portrait honourably
Hanging to the right of me.
I am not surprised
That people are sorrowful in Sutherland
Since they lost the couple
Who were harmonious, magnificent, handsome,
Earl William the Colonel
And his young spouse Mary Maxwell.

I was likening the chieftains
To a good oven that was useful
After its fire was put out,
And when only an ember remained.
O I am confident yet
That in a little time from now
That spark Betty will
Blaze into a joyous fire.

When you were an infant
And when you were lacking years,
Fortune and favour began
To restrain your enemies.
Your guardians were skilful
And the aid of Providence followed them.
Your opponents lost their expectations –
You kept your lands and your titles.

I will conclude this song,
For it is a matter too lofty for my intellect,
With one prayer for this little girl
That she should remain living as a sole memorial.
I am confident in Providence
And O God, may I see and hear
Of your marriage to a worthy man
Who will continue the customs of your forebears.

SIX

Gleann-Gallaidh, aig Ceann Loch-Eireabuill
Gleanna-Gallaidh, Gleanna-Gallaidh,
Gleanna-Gallaidh nan craobh;
Co a chi e nach mal e,
Gleanna-Gallaidh nan craobh

Ri faicinn crioch ard ain
'Ga mo bhreagadh gu taobh,
'S ann a smuainich mi fanadh
An Gleanna-Gallaidh nan craobh

Cha 'n aill leam bhur n-airgead;
'S ri bhur n-airm cha bhi mi;
Cha diult mi bhur drama,
Ach ri tuilleadh cha bhi

Ged a gheobhainn gu m' ailghios
Ceann-taile Mhic-Aoidh,
'S mor a b' annsa leam fanadh
An Gleann-Gallaidh nan craobh

Glen Golly, at the head of Loch Eriboll
Glen Golly, Glen Golly,
Glen Golly of the trees,
Who could see it and not love it,
Glen Golly of the trees.

The view of the frontier heights
Entices me yonder,
And I'm thinking I will dwell
In Glen Golly of the trees.

I don't desire your wealth
And I have no need of your weapons.
I wouldn't refuse your dram
But I require nothing else.

Even if I received for my delight
Kintail Mackay,
I would far rather dwell
In Glen Golly with its trees.

The Pipers' Appendix

Talmine Bay, composed by Pipe Major Robert Sutherland of the
Highland Light Infantry

TWO

Composed by William MacDonald, Gruids by Lairg

This tune was composed by Willie MacDonald about the 1930s.

He used to play the pipes at ceilidhs and dances. This tune was very popular with all the young people at the dances and became known as 'Willie's Polka'.

It was in great demand during the '30s, '40s, and '50s.

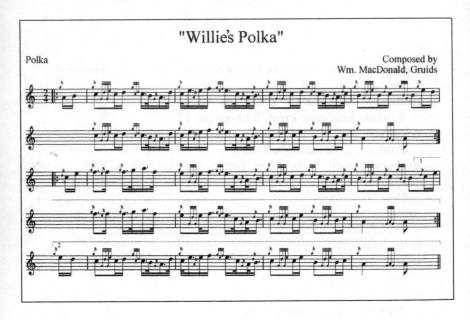

"Willie's Polka"

Polka

Composed by
Wm. MacDonald, Gruids

Bibliography

Anderson, Ian G., *Scotsmen In The Service of The Czars*, Pentland Press, Haddington, 1990

Anderson, Marjorie O., *Kings and Kingship in Early Scotland*, Scottish Academic Press, Edinburgh, 1973

Anderson, Peter D., *Robert Stewart 1533–1593*, John Donald Publishers, Edinburgh, 1982

Ascherson, Neal, *Stone Voices*, Granta Books, London, 2002

Ashley, Mike, *British Kings and Queens*, Barnes and Noble, Inc., New York, 1998

Baldwin, John R. (ed.) *The Province of Strathnaver*, The Scottish Society for Northern Studies, Edinburgh, 2000

Beith, Mary, *Healing Threads*, Polygon, Edinburgh, 1995

Boardman, Stephen, *The Early Stewart Kings*, Tuckwell Press, East Linton, 1996

Bower, Walter, *A History Book For Scots*, University of St Andrews, St Andrews, 1998

Butter, Rachel, *Kilmartin*, Kilmartin House Trust, Kilmartin, 1999

Campbell, Marion, *Argyll*, Colin Baxter, Grantown-on-Spey, 1995

Cruden, Stewart, *The Scottish Castle*, Spurbooks, Edinburgh, 1960

Devine, T. M., *The Scottish Nation 1700–2000,* Penguin, London, 1999

Dickinson, W. Croft, *Scotland from the Earliest Times to 1603,* Oxford University Press, Oxford, 1977

Donaldson, Professor Gordon, *Scottish Historical Documents,* Neil Wilson Publishing, Glasgow, Post 1993

Douglas, Kenneth, *Songs and Poems by Robert Mackay* (first edition), Inverness, 1829

Gerber, Pat, *Stone Of Destiny,* Canongate, Edinburgh, 1997

Gies, Frances and Joseph, *Daily Life in Medieval Times,* Black Dog and Leventhal Publishers, New York, 1990

Grimble, Ian, *The World of Rob Donn,* Saltire Society, Edinburgh, 1999

Grimble, Ian, *Chief Of Mackay,* Saltire Society, Edinburgh, 1993

Grimble, Ian, *The Trial of Patrick Sellar,* Saltire Society, Edinburgh, 1993

Grimble, Ian, *Clans and Chiefs,* Barnes and Noble, New York, 1980

Grimble, Ian, *The World of Rob Donn,* Edina Press, Edinburgh, 1979

Gunn, Rev. Adam and MacFarlane, Malcolm (eds) *Songs and Poems by Rob Donn Mackay,* Celtic Monthly Office, Glasgow, 1899

Houston, R. A. and Knox, W. W. J. (eds) *The New Penguin History of Scotland,* Penguin, London, 2001

Hume Brown, P., *Story of a Nation: Scotland,* Lang Syne Publishers Ltd, Glasgow, 1990

Hunter, James, *A Dance Called America,* Mainstream Publishing, Edinburgh, 1994

Lynch, Michael, *Scotland, a New History,* Pimlico, London, 2001

MacCulloch, Donald B., *Romantic Lochaber, Arisaig and Morar,* Lines Publishing, Spean Bridge, 1996

MacDonald, Charles, *Moidart Among The Clanranalds,* Birlinn, Edinburgh, 1997

Macdonald, Donald J., *Clan Donald,* Macdonald Publishers, Loanhead, 1978

MacDonald, Norman H., *The Clan Ranald Of Lochaber*, no publisher quoted.

MacDougall, M. O., *The Clan Mackay*, Johnston and Bacon Publishers, Edinburgh, 1972

MacKay, Dr James, *Pocket History of Scotland*, Parragon, Bath, 2002

Mackie, J. D., *A History of Scotland*, Penguin, London, 1964

MacKinnon, Charles, *Scottish Highlanders*, Barnes and Noble, New York, 1984

MacLean, Fitzroy, *A Concise History, Scotland*, Thames and Hudson, London, 2001

MacNie, Alan, *Clan MacDonald*, Cascade Publishing Company, Jedburgh, 1989

MacNie, Alan, *Clan Mackay*, Cascade Publishing Company, Jedburgh, 1989

Magnusson, Magnus, *Scotland: The Story of a Nation*, HarperCollins, London, 2000

Moffat, William, *A History of Scotland, 1, 2 and 3*, Oxford University Press, Oxford, 1985

Paterson, Raymond Campbell, *The Lord of the Isles*, Birlinn, Edinburgh, 2001

Pearson, Heasketh, *Johnson and Boswell*, Cassell Publishers, London, 1958

Pennick, Nigel, *The Celtic Saints*, Sterling Publishing, New York, 1997

Pittock, Murray G. H., *A New History of Scotland*, Sutton Publishing, London, 2003

Prebble, John, *Culloden*, Penguin, London, 1961

Scott, Tom, *Tales of Sir William Wallace*, Gordon Wright Publishing, Edinburgh, 1997

Scott, Tom, *Tales of King Robert The Bruce*, Gordon Wright Publishing, Edinburgh, 1969

Skene, W. F., *Chronicles of the Picts and Scots*, Edinburgh, 1867

Skene, W.F., *The Highlanders of Scotland*, London, 1836

Steel, Tom, *Scotland's Story*, Collins, Glasgow, 1984

Thomson, Derrick S. (ed.), *The Companion to Gaelic Scotland*, Gairm Publications, Glasgow, 1994

Train, Sandra, *A Memory of Strath Halladale*, no publisher quoted

Tranter, Nigel, *The Story of Scotland*, Neil Wilson Publishing, Glasgow, 2003

Tranter, Nigel, *The North East*, Hodder and Stoughton, London, 1974

Watson, Fiona, *Scotland A History 8000 BC–AD 2000*, Tempus, London, 2002

Yeoman, Peter, *Medieval Scotland*, Batsford Books, London, 1995